MW01063024

BREATHING

What To Do
When You
Can't Figure Out
What To Do

by Juanita R. Ryan
2009

Acknowledgments

I want to express my gratitude for each person who read draft manuscripts of this book. Thank you to Rachel Bird, Alice Fryling, Joyce Handler, Judi Iverson-Gilbert, Pat Lundeen, Barbara Milligan, Denise Osterman, Mary Rae and Jessica Watters. Thank you each, as well, for many years of faithful love and friendship that has helped me to keep breathing through life's toughest challenges.

My warmest gratitude to James Ryan, Peter Ryan and Heidi Weston for very useful feedback during the final writing stages. Thank you, as well, for the many ways you teach me wisdom and enrich and bless my life.

I also want to express my gratitude to all the professional helpers who have cared for me through the most significant challenges of my life. Thank you each for your generous, compassionate help. You have taught me much and brought much healing to my life.

My deepest thanks, as well, to the many people who have trusted me with their personal stories and struggles. Your honesty and courage have inspired me. Your humility has been a source of grace in my life. Your trust has been a gift to me.

My primary helper with this book and with all of life's challenges has been my husband, Dale. You have read, reread and patiently offered suggestions as this manuscript has taken shape. You have loved and supported me through all the times when I didn't know what to do. Sharing life with you is my greatest joy.

©2009 Juanita R. Ryan

ISBN: 1448686253
EAN-13: 9781448686254

Table of Contents

Introduction

There are times in life when we have no idea what to do. It is as if we are stunned. Immobilized. It may be because things are happening so quickly that we can't keep up. Often it is because a crisis has taken over our lives. Whatever the specific cause, there are times in life when we feel lost and confused.

Few of us will go through life without experiencing such times. Even those of us who are normally resourceful and resilient can find ourselves adrift and disoriented when life events threaten to overwhelm normal coping skills.

This book is about what to do in times like this—times when we don't know what to do.

I have been a therapist in private practice for more than twenty years, and have walked with many people through times of crisis. This professional experience is woven into this book, but the book is primarily personal rather than professional. These meditations were written after being diagnosed and treated for breast cancer and they reflect in many ways the particular challenges I faced during this experience. This is not, however, just a book about dealing with a medical crisis. These meditations are also deeply rooted in my long struggle to recover from the shame and fear I carried as a result of childhood trauma. And they are connected to the deep learning that came from working to do my part during a particularly difficult season in my marriage. And, finally, they reflect lessons-learned from the struggle to face my codependency with respect to our oldest son's drug addiction. Each of these very different crises involved times when I didn't know what to do, and each contributed to the hard-won but basic wisdom you will find here.

No two people are the same. No two crises are the same. So, there may be some material in this book that doesn't match your experience. The best advice I can offer about this is a bit of basic wisdom you hear frequently in the Twelve Step community: "Take what works and leave the rest." My hope is that some of what I have to offer here will be helpful to you as you face whatever challenges confront you at this time in your life.

May God grant you the strength, hope and wisdom you need for your journey.

And may your roots sink deeply in the soil of God's love.

Stay Grounded

Stay Grounded

The truth will set you free.
John 8: 23

Four days before Christmas in 2006 I had a phone appointment with my doctor. I was expecting to get the results of a breast biopsy that had been done a week earlier. At the time of the biopsy, I had been assured by the radiologist that everything looked normal, but as I sat down at the desk in my office and picked up the phone to call the doctor, adrenaline began pumping wildly through my body.

The receptionist put me through to the doctor immediately. The doctor began joking with me about finally getting the biopsy done (the equipment had broken down, and it had been necessary to reschedule the biopsy). Then she launched into a sentence I did not want to hear: "Unfortunately the results came back that you have Ductal Carcinoma In Situ. I have already scheduled an appointment for you with a surgeon at nine in the morning, the day after Christmas."

I experienced the strangest sensations as I listened to these words. An image came to my mind of wanting her to rewind and start the sentence again, but this time I wanted her to say what I wanted to hear. I wanted her to rewind so I could hear her say, "Everything is fine."

While I was working hard to not hear what I had just heard, the doctor was asking if that appointment time was possible for me. She was getting ready to hang up and move on with her busy day. But I was far from being ready to hang up. I had a thousand questions that were stacking and tangling behind the barrier of my disbelief. I asked if she would be available later to talk about this. But we were going into the holiday weekend and she was leaving town for several days. And so, without getting much information about what this diagnosis might actually mean, we said good bye.

As soon as I hung up, I called my husband who was a few miles away at his office. This was my first time to speak this strange new truth: "I have cancer." My husband was in my office with his arms around me five minutes after I hung up. I was spinning emotionally and shaking physically. But he held me, and I began to feel more grounded.

A diagnosis of cancer can mean hundreds of different things. I did not know what this particular diagnosis meant. I had no idea about prognosis or treatment. All I knew was that it felt like very bad news.

As I moved through the months of additional testing, waiting, surgery, and more waiting, I found myself repeatedly caught in a powerful and confusing temptation to believe that I did not have breast cancer. In spite of all the doctors appointments and all the conversations and emails with family and friends the diagnosis of cancer had a way of turning into something surreal.

What I noticed was that, when I resisted the truth of the diagnosis, I became more anxious. This still seems counter-intuitive to me. Most commonly we deny and minimize difficult truths in an effort to decrease the discomfort of anxiety, but when I found myself resisting the truth, my anxiety increased rather than decreased. Whenever I started thinking "It can't be" I lost my grounding and began to return to that original sensation of spinning and shaking. Whenever I would simply state the truth—"I have breast cancer and I need surgery"—I would feel my feet touch the ground again, and I would experience a sense of orientation.

As a result this became a daily mantra: "I have breast cancer, and I need to have surgery." I would say this several times a day in order to accept this reality and to stay grounded.

I also began to pray each day for God's help to stay grounded in this unpleasant truth. A diagnosis of breast cancer is a lot to take in. But it was the truth, and staying connected to the truth, no matter how painful or difficult it might be, always leads us toward freedom. Denying, avoiding or minimizing that a problem really exists leads us toward dangerous, unstable places.

During the year that our oldest son was using drugs, I experienced the contrast between the problems that denial creates and the clarity and sanity that staying grounded in reality provides. For too long we ignored what our eyes and ears told us was true. This lack of acceptance of reality—this lack of grounding—added to the problem. Because we denied the extent of the problem, we acted insanely. We acted as if we could reason with our son or as if we had some way to control his choices. It was only when we faced the painful reality that our son's drug use was beyond our control that we could make healthier choices. It was only when we stayed grounded in the reality that our son needed help which we could not provide that we were able to refocus our attention on getting help for ourselves. This, as many parents in similar circumstances have learned, is a painful process, but getting grounded in *our* need for help and focusing on *our* insane behaviors was part of what made it possible for our son to get the help he desperately needed.

All of us would prefer life to be smooth and easy, but life is not like that. At least not for very long at a time. Life is one challenge after another. Often it is several challenges at once. We don't have much control over the challenges we face but we do have some control over how we respond. A key part of that response is to stay grounded in the truth about each of life's challenges and problems. Our work is to remind ourselves regularly of the truth of the difficulties we are facing. This is the only way we can feel how deeply we need God's help and the support of others. It is the only way we will be able to do what is required of us.

When you don't know what to do…stay grounded.

Questions for reflection and discussion

1. What difficulties and challenges are you facing at this time?

2. What are you aware of experiencing physically, emotionally or spiritually as you acknowledge these difficulties?

Keep Breathing

Keep Breathing

The Lord God formed the man from the dust of the ground and breathed into his nostrils the breath of life.
Genesis 2:7

K eep Breathing. These words stood in bold lettering on a card I gave a close friend. She had just received some painful news and was very distressed. She told me several days later that she carried that card with her everywhere she went so she would be reminded to take a few slow, deep breaths several times a day.

When we experience a threat of any kind (real or perceived), our bodies have a way of taking over. Our bodies know what to do to prepare us to survive the threat. The "threat alert center" in our brain communicates not with our problem-solving cerebral cortex but with our adrenal glands. Our adrenal glands then set in place a series of biochemical responses that cause, among other things, our heart to speed up, our blood pressure to increase, our muscles to tighten and our breathing to become fast and shallow.

All of this can help us survive an immediate danger. These physical changes help us respond more quickly and more powerfully to an immediate, short-term threat. They help us fight harder and run faster.

But most of life's challenges are not short-term. Marital conflict, a child's drug abuse, healing from early trauma or difficult diagnoses like cancer are all threats that can persist for weeks and months and even for a lifetime.

As a result, many of us live in a chronic state of high alert. Many of us live as if we were under constant threat. Tense. Pressured.

We need to slow down the adrenaline surges that are set off by fear. As simple as it might seem, paying attention to how we breathe has been shown to have a powerful impact on how our bodies respond to danger.

Changing our breathing can be a kind of antidote to the constant stress our minds and bodies experience when we are afraid. Whether we are anxious about a life crisis or any of the hundreds of other things we might fear, the simple act of slowing our breathing can make a significant difference.

We cannot control most of the changes that happen in our body when a sense of threat is present. We cannot make our heart calm or our blood pressure go down, but we can slow our breathing. With a little effort, our quick, shallow breaths can be turned into slow, deep breaths. Like my friend who carried that card with her as a reminder, we need to pay attention to our breathing from time to time and slow it down a bit.

The amazing thing about this simple practice is that, when we pay attention to our breathing and begin to take some slow, deep breaths, we are sending a clear message to our bodies and brains that it is okay to relax a bit. It is like sounding the "All Clear" signal. As a result, not only does our breathing slow down but all the other physical and biochemical changes that our adrenal glands have set in motion begin to subside. It can help our heart to stop racing, our blood pressure to come down and our muscles to let go of a little of the tension they are holding.

But there is more. Gently attending to our breathing not only reduces stress on our bodies, it also soothes and nurtures our minds and spirits by grounding us in the present. When we sit quietly, even for a few minutes, and pay attention to our breathing in and breathing out, slowing it down, letting the gift of oxygen flow all the way down to our belly, we quiet our wild thoughts for a time and allow ourselves to be in our body—rather than in our fears—living in this moment, one moment at a time.

When I was working to heal from childhood trauma, I was often anxious. My nights were frequently disturbed by terrible dreams and my days were interrupted by flashbacks. In order to function, I began to practice times of slow, deep breathing every day. Often, I would begin my mornings with time alone to pray. These times usually started with five to ten minutes of slowing my breathing, relaxing my tense muscles and allowing myself to be in the present. Throughout the day I would take short breaks and allow myself a few more slow, easy breaths to calm my nerves. Breathing in this way became a survival tool for me.

It was many years after this difficult healing work that I was diagnosed with cancer. Within a few days, I returned to the regular practice of setting aside time to slow my breathing. I again added extra time each morning to my prayer times. I would begin these times with a few minutes of slow, deep breathing. Sometimes I listened to music as I breathed in this way. Sometimes I sat in silence with my hands open in a gesture of surrender and receptivity. Often I did both. These times were sacred to me. They calmed my mind and body. They helped me to stay in the moment, and they allowed me to experience times of resting in the reality of God's unfailing love.

As we pay attention to our breathing and slow it down, we can remember that with each breath we are receiving God's gift of life to us deeply, fully, one breath, one moment at a time, here, now, in this moment.

Because this is such a simple practice, it is easy to underestimate its value. And it is easy to forget to use it on a regular basis. But when we are aware of feeling anxious or tense, we can allow our discomfort to serve as a reminder to take a few, slow, deep breaths and to plan a time in the near future when we can sit quietly for a longer period of time to attend to our breathing.

When you don't know what to do…keep breathing.

Questions for reflection and discussion

1. What are you aware of feeling in your body right now?

2. Look at a watch or clock and practice taking six slow, easy breaths over a minute. Then continue for one more minute with this same rate of breathing as you reflect on the gift of life offered to you in each breath.

3. What was your experience as you slowed your breathing and reflected on the gift of life in each breath?

Gather Information

Gather Information

Listen to advice and accept instruction,
and in the end you will be wise.
Proverbs 19:20

Knowledge is power. That is what I was taught as a twenty year old nursing student. We learned to empower our patients wherever we worked by sharing information with them. Whether we were preparing people for a procedure, or for a surgery, or for having a baby, or for living with a chronic illness, one of our most important tasks was to educate people about what to expect, what choices they had, what was going on in their bodies, how to speak up for themselves, how to get support and how to take good care of themselves.

Perhaps it is because of this early training that one of my primary coping skills is to gather information. When I am faced with a difficulty in life, I gather as much information as I can so I can make informed decisions.

Because of the Internet, we now have a great deal of information at our finger tips. It is a wonderful thing. I had five days of waiting between the time I was told I had been diagnosed with cancer to the time I was scheduled to see the surgeon. During that time I read a lot.

I tried to go to the more reputable sites for information. There is a lot of misinformation on the Internet and I did not want to needlessly add to my anxiety. I also tried to read for no more than thirty minutes at a time in order to avoid information overload.

The reading yielded some helpful information. First, my particular diagnosis was considered by many professionals to be pre-cancerous. The reason for this is that *ductal carcinoma in situ* means that the abnormal cells are contained inside a duct gland. Because the abnormal cells have not spread to the surrounding area it is not considered to be a full blown cancer. This meant that my life was not in immediate danger. And it meant that I would probably not have to undergo chemotherapy.

I also learned that in spite of the fact that this was considered to be pre-cancerous it was still serious. It seemed that there was good reason to believe that these abnormal cells—which were contained in a duct gland—could break through the wall of the duct gland and mutate into a more aggressive kind of cancer if left untreated. This meant I needed to have surgery. These cells had to be removed.

Finally, I learned that the choices that were usually offered to a woman with this kind of cancer were to either have a mastectomy or to have a lumpectomy followed by five to eight weeks of daily radiation treatments. A mastectomy, of course, would mean losing a breast. Five to eight weeks of daily radiation treatment would mean fatigue, possible skin burns, some impact on the lung—although probably small—and a daily disruption in my schedule. This information was all very sobering.

All of this research helped me know what I was facing and what I was not likely to have to face. It helped me go to the appointment with the surgeon with a bit less anxiety and with more informed questions.

Having some information about whatever life challenges we are experiencing can help to reduce our anxieties. It can eliminate some of the uncertainties. It helps us better prepare ourselves.

But I needed more than facts. I also needed the kind of information that would give me emotional and spiritual strength. I found this kind of information in talking with women who had been through the experience of breast cancer. Two of my closest friends are breast cancer survivors. They offered information, emotional support, understanding, and the unspoken assurance that I would get through this and that life would return to "normal" again.

What they shared informed both my mind and my heart. They offered me hope and strength. It lit a candle in what felt like a very dark passage way.

I had seen the value of this kind of personal information sharing years earlier when I helped lead a support group for people living with cancer. Group members shared all kinds of helpful information—what to expect during different treatments, how to get through long, difficult nights, how to enjoy life as much as possible while going through such a challenging season. This level of information and support was priceless.

When I was a young nurse in training in the early 70's, attitudes about talking to people who had life-threatening diagnoses were changing rapidly. Up until that time it was not unusual to withhold information from people about the seriousness of their illness. This information was actually kept a secret from the person who most needed to know. I remember being stunned by the thought that people had once been kept in the dark about their medical conditions. They had no opportunity to get their affairs in order and no chance to say those last difficult, tender good-byes.

Some information is painful. There is a strong instinct in us to resist or avoid news we don't want to be true. When I first began to remember the traumatic events of my childhood, the instinct to resist these memories was very powerful. I had similar experiences when marital and parenting crises emerged in my life. I did not want these things to be true. I did not want more information about them, I just wanted to make them go away.

We cannot, however, face problems unless we know we have them. Gathering information is empowering because we have a better idea about our choices and about what might be required of us. Gathering information also helps us stay grounded. We need to stay closely connected to reality—whether it is painful or hopeful—because this is what leads to emotional, mental, spiritual, physical and relational health.

This is true of all problems in life—problems in our personal lives, in our families, in our society, in our world. Our work is to keep listening to the truth, and to gather both the difficult and the hopeful information about that truth, so we can bring needed correction and healing to our lives, our relationships and our world.

When you don't know what to do…gather information.

Questions for reflection and discussion

1. What information have you gathered about your situation that has been difficult to learn?

2. What information have you gathered that has given you greater hope and strength?

3. What might help you gather information without creating information overload?

Feel What You Feel

Feel What You Feel

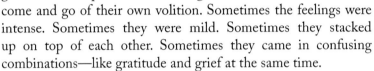

Whoever humbles himself like this little child
is the greatest in the kingdom of heaven.
Matthew 18:4

After I was diagnosed with cancer I felt everything. I felt fear. I felt shock. I felt grief. I felt shame. I felt numbness. I felt resentment. I felt jealousy. I felt anger. I felt gratitude. I felt peace. These feelings seemed to come and go of their own volition. Sometimes the feelings were intense. Sometimes they were mild. Sometimes they stacked up on top of each other. Sometimes they came in confusing combinations—like gratitude and grief at the same time.

There were times when I had the thought: "I am not doing this very well." I think this idea came when I was caught up in a feeling that I did not like. Or when I felt ashamed of a particular emotional response. I knew that my work was to stay honest about all of these feelings—and to find a way to share them with God and with a few trusted friends.

I say this was my *work* because it did not necessarily come naturally or easily to me. I resisted many of these feelings as they came unbidden into my heart and mind. My work, therefore, was to keep asking God for gifts of humility and courage to acknowledge whatever I was feeling.

Sometimes I found it helpful to view my feelings as visitors who were knocking at my heart's door. They came asking to be acknowledged and to be given a voice. They needed to find expression and to be embraced. When I was able to invite them in and listen to them they enriched my life, offered me clarity, brought me wisdom, and showed me where I needed correction.

As I prayed for the humility and courage to acknowledge my feelings and invited them in as valued visitors, I found myself expressing a wide range of emotions. There were times when I wept. Times when I wrote in my prayer journal about my fear or shame. Times when I confessed my resentments and jealousies. Times when I expressed my gratitude for the gifts I was receiving. And times when I rested in the surprising gifts of peace that came as part of the process.

One of the things that we tend to dislike about our feelings is that they are not always rational. We feel things that don't make logical sense to us. For example, my feelings of jealousy towards people who were experiencing good health—whose lives were not suddenly disrupted and out of their control—this jealousy certainly felt irrational to me. Similarly, my feelings of fear seemed irrational. The type of cancer I had was 100% treatable. It was even sometimes called a "pre-cancerous condition." But our feelings do not go away simply because we try to dismiss them as irrational. On the contrary, the more we resist them because we don't want to feel them, the more they seem to lay claim on our attention and our limited energy.

The danger is that our dislike of the irrational nature of many of our feelings can lead us to ignore or deny them. This can be very problematic. When we ignore or deny our feelings we cannot learn from them. Pushing our feelings away robs us of important opportunities to learn about ourselves, to seek support and to make needed changes. Feelings may not be rational but they have a logic of their own if we are willing to listen to them and explore them.

We do well to become like little children when it comes to our feelings. The goal is not to become children who are out of control with their feelings, but children who know it is okay to simply feel what they feel and to find ways to talk about those feelings. Such children are able to be vulnerable with others. They are able to get the help and support they need.

Recently our grandson started preschool. He is a very social child, so mostly he loves preschool. With one exception. For the first two weeks he cried every time he had to go outside for recess. He told us that he was afraid that he would be left alone on the playground when every one else went back inside.

While I was talking with him about this fear one day, I started to say what probably several other adults had already said to him. I started to say, "You know, your teacher won't leave you out on the playground." But as soon as I started to say this he stopped me. "Don't say those words!" he interjected. So I stopped and started over. "I am sorry you are feeling afraid each day on the playground," I said. "Thanks," he responded quietly.

This was a helpful reminder. When we are experiencing uncomfortable feelings, we do not need or want to be reminded that our feelings are irrational. We do not need to be talked out of them. What we do need is empathy, support and care.

Empathy with my grandson's fear opened up additional conversations. We were able to talk together about what might help him feel less afraid. Talking more about his fears, thinking of resources and strategies available to him, and acknowledging his courage seemed to calm his fears and eventually recess became the enjoyable time it was meant to be.

And so it was for me. When I felt the build up of grief and I allowed myself to cry with my husband, I was able to experience the amazing gift of comfort. I was always soothed and strengthened by this gift. And I was able to know deeply that there was nothing in this life or in death that we cannot face when we are supported, loved and comforted.

When I paid attention to my jealousy and took inventory of my resentments, I was able to face the dark thoughts inside me. The pride, the self-serving, the lack of trust, the self deceit all came forward for me to see and acknowledge. Facing and confessing these dark thoughts and feelings to God and a few others, helped me to experience the sweet breath of God's grace flowing into me, loving me and releasing me.

When I felt afraid and ran like a little child to God's loving arms, I was able to feel the compassion and empathy of God. I was able to remember that I was not alone. I was able to know again that God shepherds me, guides me, helps me. I was reminded that even when I walk through the valley of the shadow of death, I do not need to be afraid, because God is always with me.

From the gifts of comfort, soothing, strengthening, release, forgiveness, grace, reassurance, compassion—all of which were the result of expressing what I was feeling—came the experience of deep gratitude. And from the gratitude, came moments of a deep, quiet joy.

No matter what the difficulty, our feelings lead us back to our need to become like little children. Humble. Unashamed of needing help and comfort. Capable of weeping. Capable of laughing. Capable of saying, "I am sorry." Capable of learning. Capable of giving and receiving gifts of love. Capable of joy.

When you don't know what to do…feel what you feel.

Questions for reflection and discussion

1. What are some of the feelings you have been experiencing?

2. What feelings do you have about these feelings?

3. What might each of these feelings be "saying" to you?

4. What are you needing to do in response to your feelings?

Take in Support

Take in Support

Two are better than one,
because they have good return for their work.
If one falls down,
his friend can help him up.
Ecclesiastes 4:9, 10

On the evening of September 11, 2001 my husband and I watched Gwen Ifill of PBS interview Mr. Rogers. Gwen was asking Mr. Rogers to give people advice about how to talk with their children about what had just happened.

That day we had watched images of commercial jets flying into the Twin Towers in New York City, eventually collapsing the enormous structures and killing thousands trapped inside. We were shocked. We were horrified. We were traumatized. And so were our nation's children who saw these images playing over and over on television.

Mr. Rogers said that when he was a child and something very difficult happened, his mother would suggest that he notice all the helpers. And so one of the things he suggested that we do for our children (and ourselves) was to gently ask the question, "Have you seen a lot of helpers lately?"

A lot of helpers. That is what we need whenever we are experiencing something that is scary or that threatens to overwhelm us. We need a lot of helpers any time we are faced with a serious difficulty in life.

Helpers come in lots of forms. Family members. Friends. Professionals. Strangers. People close. People far away.

And the help they each offer is unique. Each one comes with their own special gift to give us. Some will be good listeners. Some will pray. Some will have experiences of their own to offer. Some will send cards. Others might email or phone. Some are skilled professionals who will treat the problem. They each come with their own precious gifts. Gifts that tell us that we matter, that we are not alone, that we are loved.

Our work is to receive these gifts of support and care. As simple as that sounds, it is often difficult to do. Receiving support and care from others requires honesty and humility. We cannot receive while we are pretending that we are fine. Receiving requires us to acknowledge our need for helpers.

In my roles as a nurse and as a therapist I am a professional helper. I know from personal experience that professional helpers are sometimes especially resistant to being on the receiving end of love and care. There are many reasons why it is difficult for professional helpers to stay open to receiving care. When we are in the role of helper we feel okay about ourselves. We may feel in control. We may feel competent or capable. All of these feelings are more pleasant than the feelings which come when we are needy or afraid.

It is not just professional helpers who have difficulty with receiving help from others. We all do. Whether we are a professional helper or not, the good feelings that come from giving and doing and looking good are easier for us—and less threatening to our pride. So, any of us can hide behind our giving and doing for others. And we can, tragically, do more harm than good when the primary drive behind our helping and giving and doing is to bolster our own sense of value.

Being on the receiving end of help and care is not easy for most of us because when we are in need we don't feel in control, we don't feel powerful, we feel that we don't have anything to offer, or we experience ourselves as less than competent. Instead, we feel our need, our dependency on others, our powerlessness, our vulnerability.

Receiving may not be easy for all of these reasons. But receiving care and support from others is good for us. It offers us the gift of humility. And it offers us the opportunity to experience in practical ways that we are valued.

What is particularly significant is that this experience of being valued does not come because of something we are doing. The experience of being valued when we are most in need of support is the experience of being valued simply because we are. We matter. Others care about us.

This is a very powerful gift. It is a gift that gives us the strength we need to get through each day whatever the difficulty we are facing. Sometimes we will experience this strengthening spiritually, sometimes emotionally, sometimes physically.

While I waited in the preoperative area for my second surgery, I listened to music and took long, slow, easy breaths. My heart rate which is normally about sixty beats a minute was showing on the monitor as only forty eight beats per minute. So at a time when it is common to be anxious, the music and slow easy breathing and the prayers of many others were all keeping me in a peaceful place.

There were, however, a few moments before my husband was allowed to join me in the preoperative area during which my peaceful state was interrupted with a rush of anxiety that made me feel a bit dizzy. I suddenly experienced a need to have someone I knew and loved physically present with me.

When my husband was able to join me, he pulled up a chair next to the bed and took my hand. At that moment the peace returned and stayed. Even when he wasn't actually holding my hand, when he was simply there with me, I felt physically supported and emotionally comforted.

Both of my surgeries took place during the Lenten season. Lent is the seven weeks between Ash Wednesday and Good Friday—a time when I usually reflect with greater frequency on the gift of Jesus' life and death. For the first time I felt like I got a small glimpse of what it might have meant to Jesus to have a few loved ones close by as he died. I suspect that he was deeply comforted by their presence. I imagine that he felt held, in some way, by being able to see their eyes and hear their voices.

It is hard to describe the physical comfort that comes from the quiet, loving presence of another person. When the surge of anxiety hit me before my husband joined me that day, I felt for an instant like I might somehow physically fly apart. It was a strange sensation. When my husband came and sat with me, I felt physically held together.

Experiences like this are, I think, a reflection of our deep connection with one another. None of us exists alone. None of us can live life alone. We need each other.

I felt such gratitude for every kind word and gentle touch offered by the many health care professionals I encountered. The smallest kindness can touch deep places inside us when we are so vulnerable.

I kept every card people sent me. I even kept a few voice mails of love and support. I knew that I needed to drink in these gifts. I needed to take in this sweet soul nurture from those who offered themselves to me at a vulnerable time.

My prayer is that the deeper opening that this crisis created in my heart will stay open. My prayer is that every day I will be freed to humbly, joyfully remember my need for the support and care of others. My prayer is that I will be given the grace to receive all the love and support that is offered to me each day, whatever the day may hold.

When you don't know what to do...take in support.

Questions for reflection and discussion

1. What support have you been offered during your times of difficulty?

2. What is it like for you to take in that support?

3. What do you need to do to reach out for further support?

Pray

Pray

Trust in him at all times, O people;
pour out your hearts to him,
for God is our refuge.
Psalm 62:8

When we are faced with difficulties in life, we need support from friends and family. We also need God's help. Perhaps the most direct way to open ourselves to God is through prayer.

Prayer can be many things.

Prayer does not need to be long or complicated. When we are afraid or distressed we need to be able to talk to God directly and honestly. When we are experiencing difficulties, we need the freedom to pray in ways that are urgent and to the point. During difficult times our prayers may come in short gasps: "Help!" or "Show me what to do!"

Sometimes even praying short, urgent prayers can be more than we can do. Sometimes we have to rely on others who are praying on our behalf. And sometimes we have no words and have to let our prayer be the prayer of resting silently in God's loving arms.

Many years ago, our oldest son dropped out of high school and started using drugs. I was in a state of codependent panic much of the time. A good friend prayed for me and asked God if there might be some message she could pass on to me. My friend had a strong sense of hearing God say one word. "Rest."

When my friend relayed this word to me I was startled. Our son was not doing well. I was distraught and afraid. I was in full-alert mode, ready 24/7 to do whatever needed to be done. But the invitation was to rest.

Over time I have come to see the invitation to rest as an invitation to a very deep kind of prayer. It is the prayer of trust. It is the prayer of a young child who is afraid or overwhelmed and finds comfort and strength by curling up in their parent's loving, protective arms.

The way this kind of prayer has worked for me has been very visual. I see and feel myself as a small child, held in Jesus' arms. Sometimes I sit quietly with this image, allowing my body, my heart, my mind and my soul to be at rest. And sometimes I carry this image with me as I work or drive, allowing this silent prayer to soothe and sustain me.

Long before I was diagnosed with cancer, I helped lead a cancer support group. There were times when a group member would comment that they just could not pray. They felt too sick, or too exhausted to pray. Often they would report that their experience during these times was of being held by grace. All their lives they had been striving hard to pray "right" and believe "just right" in order to please God. Now all they could do was be. All they could do was rest in the reality that God was with them, that God was caring for them. And in this way they came to experience God's love and grace in ways they had never been open to experiencing before.

It is my practice to write in a prayer journal almost every day. This writing is personal, private and honest. I tell God what I am feeling, what I am needing, where I see myself failing, what I am grateful for. I invite God to show me more about ways in which I need to be corrected or healed. I ask for wisdom and guidance for my day. I give myself, my day, my worries to God. I share my gratitude for all the gifts I have received. And I express my love and affection for God.

Pouring out my heart to God in this way helps to keep me more honest and more grounded. And it helps me stay in a place of humility. Prayer is an act of humility. It is an acknowledgment that we are creatures—that we are dependent on our Creator. It reminds us that we are not God. It reminds us that we are not in charge.

This kind of dependency is not easy for most of us. We live in a culture that values independence, self-sufficiency, doing for oneself. We minimize the reality of our deep interdependence, as neighborhood communities, as national communities and as a global community. And we minimize our dependence on God— for life, for breath, for help and care of every kind.

Many of us struggle with deep shame for having a need we cannot meet by ourselves. Being dependent and in need of help or support feels shameful. This kind of shame often has its roots in childhood experiences of neglect or abuse. If our needs and natural dependency were not responded to with support and respect, we may have come to the conclusion that it is a bad and shameful thing to need others or to need God.

The truth is that we need each other and we need God. God does not shame us for our needs, instead God welcomes us and all of our needs.

An exercise that has been very helpful to me when I have gone through difficult times has been to read through the Psalms. This was especially powerful for me during the years when I was processing the raw pain that I carried as a result of childhood trauma. The Psalms helped me find the words of need and longing that my shame wanted to hold back. The psalmists do not hold back anything out of shame. They pour out their hearts and souls to God. The fear, the anger, the need for help of every kind, the longing for relationship with God, the gratitude for God's love and care, the joy. It is all there.

The psalmists teach us that we can "call on God in the day of trouble" and that God will respond with the love, the strength, the compassion and the help we need.

Whether our prayer is a gasp, an outpouring of our hearts, a quiet resting in God, or a simple trust that others are praying for us, it is a blessed thing to pray.

When you don't know what to do…pray.

Questions for reflection and discussion

1. What is it like for you to pray when things are going smoothly?

2. What has it been like for you to pray during a time of difficulty?

3. What are you most needing from God today?

Practice Surrender

Practice Surrender

Do not be anxious about anything,
but in everything, by prayer and petition,
with thanksgiving, present your requests to God.
And the peace of God,
which transcends all understanding,
will guard your hearts
and your minds in Christ Jesus.
Philippians 4: 6, 7

A few weeks after I was diagnosed with cancer, a music CD arrived in the mail from a friend. Several years earlier this friend had been told she had ovarian cancer and needed surgery. It turned out to be a false alarm, but she'd had a deeply significant spiritual experience through her ordeal. This music had been a great help to her and she wanted to share it with me.

One particular track on the CD caught my attention. A single female voice, without accompaniment, sings with quiet strength. The music and words are simple. "Into thy hands, I commit myself. Into thy hands, I entrust all I am and all that holds my heart. Into thy hands, I commit."[1] These words are repeated over and over by a growing chorus of voices.

The lyrics speak about surrender. Not about giving up. Not about resignation. But about a surrender to love.

Like many of us, I mostly want to believe that I am in charge of things. I want to believe that I have the power to manage just about everything—including my health and my life. I want to control what I cannot control. The truth is that I did not give myself life. I do not sustain my life. My life—every moment of it—is a gift. It is given to me by a creating, giving God.

When I try to control things that are out of my control, I create needless stress and anxiety for myself. But when I acknowledge that my life—each day, each breath—is a gift, I can begin to entrust "myself…all I am and all that holds my heart" into God's loving care.

Trust, it turns out, is not an easy thing to do.

It is not easy to trust a God we have not seen. It is not easy to trust that God is loving enough or powerful enough to take good care of us. It is not easy to open our clenched fists and let go of all we want to control.

Many years earlier I struggled with other difficult issues including trying to find ways to heal our strained marriage. As I prayed for help and guidance, a simple image came to me. In this image I saw life as a large, quickly flowing river. I was in a small boat, floating on this river. There was no way to steer the small boat. My instinct was to try to reach up and grab onto the branches of trees that hung over the water. I wanted to stop what was happening. I wanted to be able to take charge of what was going on. But it wasn't possible. The branches were out of my reach no matter how hard I stretched. The situation was pretty clear: I could either keep trying to find a way to take control of things that I could not control, or I could recline in the boat, allow myself to rest and experience the ride.

As I stayed with this image and stopped trying to grab onto the passing branches—as I allowed myself to sit back in the boat and relax—I had a growing sense that the boat was actually God's hand carrying me. It was God's hand carrying me through life. All of life. Both the smooth places and the white-water rapids.

The same God who made me, the God who sent Jesus to reveal God's amazing love, the God who gives me breath, this One is carrying me. I am in God's hands. I am safe. I am held. So I can stop all my controlling and striving and thrashing about. I can entrust myself and all that holds my heart to God's loving care.

We are not meant to live in reliance on our own strength, brain power and willpower. The entire adventure of life is meant to be lived in reliance on our Creator. Life is meant to be an experience of communion, even union with God, in which we open ourselves to God—to the One who is Wisdom, Love, Grace, Guidance, Peace, Life, Light and Joy. Life is meant to be an experience, not of going it alone, but of going with God.

This image of resting in the palm of God's hand—the "letting go and letting God" experience—could imply a kind of passivity. But there is nothing passive about surrendering to God's love. Surrender does not mean we do nothing. It means that we do everything in reliance on God.

The practice of "letting God be God" is a kind of surrender to love that requires an ongoing, daily practice. My experience is that when I am anxious or afraid, I always want to take back control. The times I most need to entrust myself to God's care are the very times I instinctively try to control what I cannot control. I have found that anytime I am anxious or angry, I need to stop and open my hands and heart in prayer. Anxiety and anger have become signals to me that I need to be honest with God about all that I am feeling and to entrust myself, my fears, my needs, my resentments, my concerns, my requests to God's care.

What I observed after being diagnosed with breast cancer was that I would frequently tense up. If I would pause to pay attention to this, I would usually find that I was anxious about the next event—the next test, the next surgery, or the next set of results that were coming. I was bracing myself. I was resisting the ride. But when I was able to reconnect with my dependence on God, it was as if I was able to lean back and rest again in God's loving hand.

Anytime we are afraid or in distress, we can allow ourselves to stop and hear God saying, like a loving parent: "You don't have to be afraid. I am right here with you. Tell me what you need. I will help you." Then, as trusting children, we can surrender. We can say "Okay" and let go and entrust ourselves to God's good care.

When you don't know what to do…practice surrender.

Questions for reflection and discussion

1. What thoughts and feelings do you have about the image of surrender or of resting in God's hand?

2. What things do you find most difficult to entrust to God's care?

3. What helps you to rest in God's love and care for you?

Notice Your Reactivity

Notice Your Reactivity

The fruit of the Spirit is love,
joy, peace, patience, kindness, goodness,
faithfulness, gentleness and self control.
Galatians 5:22

The first responses I received when I told people about being diagnosed with cancer were usually responses of shock and compassion. I felt tenderness from most people. And I was soothed by that tenderness.

Within days, however, I wrote in my journal that I was feeling that somehow too many of the interactions I was experiencing about my cancer seemed "off." People could not say the right thing or have the right tone. People didn't call or send cards. Or they did. Either way, I might have some reaction. I even wrote in my prayer journal that I realized I was reacting negatively to other peoples' expressions of sympathy. I didn't like hearing or seeing their sympathy. Perhaps it made my cancer diagnosis too real. "Something is wrong with me," I wrote.

I was emotionally raw. I was riding on emotional white water rapids. I was suddenly uncertain about many things I usually took for granted. And I was afraid.

When we are faced with a scary situation that continues for some time, we often become reactive. We cannot always talk ourselves out of this reactivity, but it is helpful if we at least know what is happening. Being aware that we are raw and reactive can help us to be more mindful and more prayerful about how we go about expressing our reactivity.

People who are recovering from addictions of various kinds are at risk of relapse. Some people believe that when a person is hungry, angry, lonely or tired they are at even greater risk of relapse. This can be remembered with the acronym, HALT. The idea is that a person will be less likely to relapse if they halt and pay attention to these basic concerns. People are reminded to get something to eat when they are hungry, to get some quality rest when they are tired, to make a phone call or go to a meeting when they are lonely, and to take responsibility for their feelings when they are angry.

I think this wisdom can be applied to our tendency to react when we are distressed or afraid. Not all of us will be tempted to pour ourselves a drink, but we might do something just as counter productive. We might tell people off, or withdraw from people who care about us.

Before we attack or withdraw, we do well to HALT. Then we need to take care of ourselves. We need to eat, rest and connect with someone who is supportive. We also need take responsibility for our reactions. We need to remember that we are raw and we need to remind ourselves that the people we are reacting to are people who care about us, even if they are not able to always express that care in ways that are helpful to us.

There were a few times I told myself to sleep on it, before I told someone how "hurt" I was. If the sleep didn't calm my reactivity, I spent time asking God for wisdom. I asked God to show me whether this event was something I needed to let go of or whether it was something I needed to talk through with the other person. Only once or twice was there something that needed to be talked through. Mostly, I needed to ask for grace and comfort from God and let it go.

Many years before being diagnosed with cancer I went through a long period in which I felt emotionally raw while I came to terms with childhood trauma. I would, at times, be thrown back into the feelings which I had experienced as a child—but which I could not express at that time. During those times of wanting to do the equivalent of throwing temper tantrums, I came across a helpful piece of advice from Thomas Merton. Merton said that we do well to not inflict our suffering on others. It is wise advice. I do not want to inflict my suffering on others.

So, what to do? In addition to using HALT and praying for God's comfort, grace and wisdom, I found it helpful to remember that self control is a gift of the Spirit. As we invite God's Spirit to live in us, as we surrender our wills and our lives to God's care, the life of the Spirit begins to flow through us more freely.

This requires us to practice the basic disciplines that help us with reactivity to any life event. Stay grounded. Keep breathing. Feel what we feel. Pray. Practice surrender. Set aside extra time each day to be quiet in order to practice these basics. In this way we are often able to receive the comfort and correction we need. In this way we can invite God's Spirit to flow into us and through us, giving us the gifts of self control that we need.

When you don't know what to do…notice your reactivity.

Questions for reflection and discussion

1. What have you noticed about your own reactivity?

2. Which of the suggestions made here have you tried and how did they work?

3. Which of these suggestions might be especially helpful for you?

Realize This is Happening
To Everyone in Your Life

Realize This Is Happening To Everyone In Your Life

Just as you share in our sufferings,
so also you share in our comfort.
II Corinthians 1:7

A diagnosis of cancer can have a way of immediately drawing a person into a place of fear. Fear for one's life, fear for one's health and well being, fear of loss of control and fear of the unknown may all surface. All this fear left me rather self-focused. A very big event is suddenly taking place in my life and in my body, demanding my full attention.

I could feel my focus shifting after I was diagnosed with cancer. I became myopic, seeing only what was close at hand. This big thing was happening to me! That is how it seemed to my limited eyes. The truth was that this big thing was happening to my husband, to my kids, to my extended family, to my friends, to my clients, even to people I did not know very well. I was in shock. They were in shock. I was afraid. They were afraid. This diagnosis raised issues for me. It also raised issues for each of them. I struggled with unhealthy ways of coping. They struggled with unhealthy ways of coping.

As a result, the people I relied on for support were sometimes numb to the situation and unresponsive to my needs. Sometimes they said things that were expressions of their own anxieties and were not at all helpful to me. I struggled with confusion and hurt over all of this.

But, by God's grace, I was soon able to see that in some very real ways this breast cancer was not just *my* breast cancer. This breast cancer was happening to all of us. I was the one who had to go through the tests, the surgeries and the treatments. But at least it was reasonably clear what I was supposed to do. What other people were supposed to do was less obvious, less concrete. That left people sometimes feeling helpless and anxious.

Everyone had their own way of dealing with their anxiety. One of my closest friends, someone I could always turn to and always trust, said some things that I experienced as surprisingly hurtful. She seemed a thousand miles away. I asked God to show me what to do because I could feel myself wanting to withdraw.

One day, through tears, I told her that I was wondering if she was feeling a lot of anxiety about my cancer and if that was why she seemed distant. With this friend, that was all that was needed. In an instant she was in tears, saying "I don't want this to be happening to you. I want to make this go away. And I can't. So I think I have gone away. I am sorry."

I did not have conversations like this with many people. Mostly, I needed to begin to learn from my friend's words about what other people in my life were experiencing. As I began to accept that this event was happening to everyone in my life, I was able to make room for other people's fears and numbness and denial and protective distance. This made it possible to better accept their gifts of love and support and kindness when they were able to offer them.

I was also able to see that there were some things that people in my life needed from me. They needed me to take care of myself, to give them some room to struggle with their own reactions to my struggle, and to receive their love for me.

What I experienced is true of much of life. Nothing happens to us alone. Whatever is going on in our lives always impacts many others. If we are hurt, the hurt is ours and it belongs to others as well. If we are experiencing joy, the joy is ours and it also belongs to others. If we are making destructive choices, other people are impacted. If we are making healthy choices, other people benefit.

It is not unusual for a person seeking counseling to feel that getting help for themselves is somehow selfish. People often feel that they are talking too much about themselves and thinking too much about their problems. Usually people who struggle with this are people who have spent their lives focused on other people's needs and feelings and who have spent little, if any, time exploring their own.

I always tell people who express this kind of distress that seeking help for themselves is not selfish. It is a gift to the people in their lives. In fact, it is always a gift to the people in our lives when we do anything to take care of ourselves or to bring healing and positive change in our lives. After my husband and I had worked hard in marriage therapy and found healing in our relationship, our oldest son thanked us. "Thank you for doing the work and sticking with it," he said. "You greatly improved the quality of my life."

The state of our marriage. My breast cancer. Our lives, and the events in our lives, do not belong to us alone. No one stands or falls alone. We are deeply connected to each another. We are family.

When you don't know what to do…realize that this is happening to everyone in your life.

Questions for reflection and discussion

1. Who else is being impacted directly or indirectly by the difficulty you are going through?

2. In what ways is it useful for you to remember that this situation is impacting others as well as you?

Take Inventory

Take Inventory

Search me, O God, and know my heart;
test me and know my anxious thoughts.
See if there is an offensive way in me,
and lead me in the way everlasting.
Psalm 139:25-26

Difficulties in life bring out the best in us. And the worst. This was certainly true of my experience with cancer. I prayed and practiced surrender and took in the love and support of others and of God. And I was resentful and jealous and reactive.

The resentfulness, jealousy and reactivity were not pretty. They were dark and disturbing. This darkness needed my attention. It needed to be acknowledged and healed.

Scripture offers us tools for attending to our dark side. Scripture teaches us to invite God to search us and to show us our hearts, our anxious thoughts, our offensive ways (Psalm 139:25-26). It also teaches us that confession is an important part of our healing. (James 5:16).

God is not surprised by the darkness of my responses. God knows that my self-seeking and selfishness will show itself on a regular basis. And God has provided not only forgiveness but practical help and healing. God offers to reveal my offensive ways to me and to help me tell the truth about them so that I can be healed.

The book *Alcoholics Anonymous* provides some practical tools for attending to our resentments and fears. These tools can be helpful to anyone whether we are struggling with an addiction or not. In Step Four of the Twelve Steps we are given guidelines for making a "fearless moral inventory," in which we explore our resentments and fears. And in Step Ten we continue taking daily inventory of our resentments and fears and we continue to make amends when we have wronged another person.

When I found myself reacting to the diagnosis of cancer, I used the tools of inventory taking. I began by praying that God would reveal my anxious thoughts and offensive ways. And then I wrote down what or who I was resentful towards. And why. I wrote down the ways I believed I was being hurt or threatened. And then I asked the question suggested in *Alcoholics Anonymous*: "Where was I being selfish, self-seeking, dishonest and afraid?".

The following is some of my inventory about my resentment towards friends who didn't respond just the way I wanted them to respond.

Where am I being selfish?
I think it is all about me, 'I have breast cancer, pay attention to me,' is what I seem to want to demand of my friends.

Where am I being self seeking?
I am seeking attention and sympathy, but not too much sympathy, everyone has to get it just right. I am also seeking approval for how I am handling this.

Where am I being dishonest?
I am deceiving myself in thinking that others need to pay extra attention to me; I am deceiving myself that there is a good way, as opposed to a bad way, to be coping with a difficult diagnosis; I am deceiving myself that I need to prove myself to my friends in some way; and I am forgetting the truth that I can rest in God's love and care no matter what I am feeling or needing.

Where am I afraid?
I am afraid that I am not handling this well and that I will lose the respect of my friends.

I also wrote inventory about my resentment toward the cancer itself.

Where was I being selfish?
I acknowledged the terrible thought that "I would rather this was happening to someone else instead of to me."

Where was I being self-seeking?
I would rather be the helper than the one being helped, because then I could feel more in charge of things, and feel like I have something to offer, rather than feeling out of control and vulnerable.

Where was I being dishonest?
I am believing the lie that I am in charge of my health. And I am believing the lie that I should somehow be immune from this kind of human suffering. I am also believing the lie that I don't have a lot I need to learn from this experience.

Where was I being afraid?
I am afraid the cancer might return. I am afraid of the procedures and the surgery. And I am afraid of being afraid.

After I wrote this inventory, I talked to God about what I had written and I talked to at least one other person. This was helpful. It relieved me of some of the burden of pride and pretense. I experienced some relief from the feelings that accompanied these selfish, deceitful, fearful thoughts. This is consistent with the teaching in 1 John 1:9 that when we confess our sins we are forgiven and purified. Later, in this same text (I John 2:8) it describes the "darkness passing" and the "true light shining." This is what I experienced when I took my inventory and shared it with both God and another person. I felt the darkness passing and the light of God's grace shining in me—correcting me, healing me, freeing me.

One of the reasons taking inventory is so important is that we tend to wander off the path. We forget who we are, who our neighbor is and who God is. We forget we are loved. We forget we are valued. We forget our neighbor is also deeply loved and valued. We forget that God loves us. We wander off looking for love and valuing in some other place. We get proud, greedy and defensive. We treat others as less than the precious children of God that they are. We forget that we can rest in God's love and care for us. And, as a result, we make a mess of things.

In the daily adventures of life, taking inventory of our anxious thoughts and offensive ways makes it possible for God to heal us and free us. God restores us to our right mind. God reminds us who we are, who our neighbor is and who God is. We, who were confused and lost, are found again. And, we are told, that when the lost are found, there is always great rejoicing in heaven.

When you don't know what to do...take inventory.

Questions for reflection and discussion

1. Ask God to reveal your resentments, especially in relation to the difficulty you are experiencing.

2. Who or what are you resentful toward? Why?

3. Ask God to show you, in relation to your resentments, where you are being selfish, self-seeking, dishonest or afraid.

4. Share what you have been shown with God and at least one other trusted person.

5. Ask God to continue to free you from your resentments.

Let Go Of Shame

Let Go of Shame

Let us fix our eyes on Jesus
the author and perfecter of our faith,
who for the joy set before him
endured the cross, scorning the shame.
Hebrews 12:2

S hame is that terrible, private feeling that something is wrong with us—that we are somehow defective as a person. That we are irreparably damaged. That if anyone really knew what we were like we would be rejected.

A part of the experience of shame is the fear of being found out and exposed. We want to run and hide and protect ourselves from exposure to other people's judgement.

Many of us start accumulating shame in childhood. Sometimes the roots of shame involve abuse, neglect or significant trauma. But shame can also be rooted in less intense experiences. Shame can be created if a child is told she is irresponsible or stupid when he spills his milk or brings home grades that don't meet a parent's expectations. Rather than being taught how to clean up the spilled milk, or helped in ways that might allow for greater success in school, a kind of character assassination takes place which leaves a child believing terrible things about herself.

Shame can also be formed when a child's basic needs for secure attachment, nurture and attention are chronically unmet. When our longings for relatedness are not met, the basic human need to love and to be loved can feel shameful to us.

Unfortunately, accumulated shame does not just go away as time passes. Unless it is addressed directly, we carry shame with us. Sometimes it may seem dormant, but in times of stress our shame can float to the surface of our lives and complicate things. For example, a diagnosis of a serious illness can be a trigger for feelings of shame. Being told "something is seriously wrong with you" can feel very much like the old shaming message of "you are defective" or "you can't do anything right." And when a serious diagnosis is public information we can feel very vulnerable and exposed. As a result it can be difficult to sort out our responses to the current crisis from our responses to old, accumulated shame.

The good news is that anytime shame surfaces there is an opportunity to experience healing of the experiences and beliefs that have fed the shame.

When Jesus faced death by crucifixion, we are told that he "endured the cross and scorned the shame" (Hebrews 12:2), Jesus endured the pain. That is, Jesus did not avoid the suffering, but instead, he went through the suffering. But he rejected the shame. All the shame that others were attempting to heap on him had no power over him. Jesus did not accept the shame others were trying to put on him. He was being treated as a person with little or no value. But the message of shame, "you have little or no value," was a lie and Jesus refused to accept it.

We tend to do the opposite of what Jesus did when faced with suffering. Jesus accepted suffering and rejected shame. We tend to reject the suffering—we deny it, run from it, tune it out—but we tend to embrace the shame as if it were the truth. Shame, however, is a lie. None of us is ever "less than." None of us are unlovable, beyond repair, or worthless. We are loved and cherished by a redeeming, healing, saving God. And none of us is in the wrong for longing for love and connection. This longing, although it may be painful at times, is a gift from God. It is a gift that keeps us moving toward relationship with God and with each other.

I experienced moments of shame for having breast cancer. I had feelings of being somehow "less than" women who did not have breast cancer. I had thoughts of being "marked" and "unlucky" and inferior because of this diagnosis.

When I remembered the women I know who are breast cancer survivors I could see that I was being entirely irrational. These women are some of the most beautiful humans I know.

The most important thing for me was not to figure out where these feelings of shame were coming from. The most important thing for me was to let them go.

Years earlier I had decided to practice an unusual "giving up" for the Lenten season. In some traditions it is common to make some kind of personal sacrifice in the weeks leading up to Easter that will help keep us mindful of Christ's sacrifice. I had given up desserts and chocolate on previous years. But this time I decided instead to give up my fear and shame. My sons were young at the time, and when I talked at the dinner table about my plan they asked, "You aren't going to feel any fear or shame for seven weeks?" I told them that was not my plan. I expected to continue feeling fear and shame. My plan was to stay aware of these feelings and to do my best to release them to God as soon as I was aware of them. I wasn't planning on examining them and analyzing them. I simply was going to tell God, "I am feeling fear or shame, and I release these feelings to you."

I did this practice of letting go of fear and shame for seven weeks. It changed something in me. Of course, I still experience these feelings, but I am more aware of them, and I can release them more readily.

When our family went to family week at the addiction treatment center where our son was being treated, they taught us to discard shame using a physical gesture of throwing our hands in the air and saying, "I release this shame, this shame does not belong to me." This was close to what I had done for seven weeks. Sometimes I did this outwardly with a physical gesture. Sometimes I did it inwardly. A physical gesture such as this, which symbolizes the release of shame, can be a powerful way to reinforce our growing willingness to let go of shame.

Letting go of shame is important because shame leads only to destructive places. Shame keeps us focused on how bad we feel about ourselves, and thus less aware and open to others. Shame keeps us immobilized because it is based in the belief that we are hopelessly beyond help. Shame pushes us to isolate because we feel too exposed. Shame feels so terrible that it opens the door to rage. We cannot stand to feel so terrible so we lash out at ourselves and we lash out at others.

When hard times come, feelings of shame often surface—feelings of being worthless and unlovable. We can let these feelings go. They do not belong to us. We are valued. We are loved.

When you don't know what to do…let go of shame.

Questions for reflection and discussion

1. What shame are you feeling in relation to the difficulty you are experiencing?

2. What other shame are you aware of?

3. Practice letting go of shame, throwing your hands in the air and saying, "This shame does not belong to me."

4. Ask God to help you reject the shame you feel and to be open in new ways of resting in God's love.

Extend Grace

Extend Grace

Be completely humble
and gentle; be patient;
bearing with one another in love.
Ephesians 4:2

I lost a few nights sleep in the month after being diagnosed with cancer. Usually the sleeplessness was not about my reaction to the diagnosis itself. It was because I was reacting to something friends did or didn't do. Or to something a health care professional said or didn't say. I didn't like being reactive in this way. I wanted to be humble, gentle, patient and loving all the time. But I was not. Pride, anger and impatience were often part of my struggle.

I am convinced that it is God's desire to transform us into people capable of humility, gentleness and patience. Another way of saying this is that God wants to free us from all that prevents us from reflecting the light and love of God. God's desire is to make us capable of extending grace.

When I found myself reacting to other people I prayed: "Please show me how this looks through your eyes. I know my perspective is warped because I am anxious and raw. Open my eyes and my heart."

Often praying in this way was helpful in restoring a humble, gentle perspective—an ability to extend grace. In addition to receiving grace to extend grace, my eyes were opened to see more clearly the many acts of kindness that were extended to me. As I learned to receive these gifts of kindness and allowed this grace to move me, it became easier for me to stay in a place of extending grace to others.

Often what I would see is that the friend who had said something I reacted to loved me and had no idea that what they said had been hurtful to me. What I needed was to "bear with them in love." I needed to see their love for me and my love for them and to let the missteps go.

When God gives us the grace to receive grace and to extend grace, the circle becomes complete, and we often experience the blessing of grace coming back to us. This completion of the cycle of grace does not necessarily come in the form of a direct response from people to whom we have extended grace. The completion often comes because extending grace to others creates a greater opening for the outpouring of God's love and goodness in our hearts.

The surgeon I saw is a hard working, energetic, gifted woman. I saw her for consultations twice before my first surgery and again after each of my two surgeries. One of these appointments was scheduled on a Friday late afternoon just before my first surgery. I had cleared my own work schedule so that my husband and I could get there on time. We waited for an hour and a half. We both felt a bit of the frustration that can come when you make an effort to get somewhere on time, only to find yourself waiting.

The walls were fairly thin in the consultation room where we waited and we could hear the surgeon's voice in the next room. We couldn't hear much of what was being said, but we knew she was talking to a young woman who had serious breast cancer and was very distressed.

It was not hard to extend grace for an hour and a half to the doctor. She was answering question after question and offering much needed hope and reassurance to this young women and her family. We were grateful that she was that kind of doctor.

When she came in to see us she apologized profusely. She stated briefly that it had been a heart wrenching week with too many women in their twenties and thirties faced with difficult diagnoses.

Several weeks later, after my second surgery, I was again waiting for a consultation with this surgeon. This time I had a book with me, just in case the wait was another long one. The book I had with me was Rachel Remen's *Kitchen Table Wisdom*—a deeply moving book about faith and hope in the midst of health crises. [2]

This wait turned out to be another long one, but, perhaps because of the book I was reading and the grace that flowed from it, and because I was now cancer free and done with all treatment, I was in a very calm and meditative place. I read a story from Rachel's book, and then I prayed for the surgeon. I reflected on the patience, kindness and gentleness she had extended to me. I thanked God for her and asked God to bless her richly for all she gave of herself to me and all the women she helped. And then I would read another story and pray for her again. I did this over and over for almost ninety minutes.

When she arrived and apologized again for the long delay, I felt nothing but gratitude for her. When I thanked her for all her good care for me, she put her arms around me as I sat on the end of the examination table and hugged me. As she let go of me and pulled back, her eyes were brimming with tears. I don't know what her tears were about. But I do know that grace filled the room, holding us both in its kind embrace.

When things are tough, ask for grace to extend grace. Then wait and watch. Grace will flow to you, through you and right back at you.

When you don't know what to do...extend grace.

Questions for reflection and discussion

1. Who has extended grace to you during this and other difficult times?

2. To whom have you extended grace during this difficult time?

3. What was the experience like for you to give or receive grace?

Show Up

Show Up

Let us not become weary in doing good.
Galatians 6:9

Sometimes life is mostly about showing up. And sometimes that is not easy to do. My experience with cancer, much like my experience of healing from childhood trauma, was a long series of needing to show up. Showing up to take care of cancer means showing up for doctor's appointments, tests and surgeries. In addition to these events, I was preparing myself for the possibility that I might need to show up five days a week for seven weeks of radiation treatment. None of this felt easy to me.

Henri Nouwen, in his book *The Path of Waiting*, writes about spending time with a man who was in the late stages of cancer. This man had been active in ministry all his life. He was a doer. Now he could no longer do. Instead, he was the recipient of other peoples' doing. Nouwen writes about their exploration of this challenge together and ends with a meditation on the phrase that Scripture uses in connection with the final stages of Jesus' life. It is the expression: "being handed over."

> The term 'to be handed over' plays a central role in the life of Jesus. Indeed, this drama of being handed over divides the life of Jesus radically in two. The first part of Jesus' life is filled with activity....But immediately after Jesus is handed over, he becomes the one to whom things are being done...It is important for us to realize that when Jesus says, "It is accomplished" (John 19:30), he does not simply mean, "I have done all the things I wanted to do." He also means, "I have allowed things to be done to me that needed to be done to me in order for me to fulfill my vocation.".... He doesn't just fulfill his vocation by doing the things

the Father sent him to do, but also by letting things be done to him that the Father allows to be done to him. Passion is a kind of waiting—waiting for what other people are going to do....It is in the passion that the fullness of God's love shines through. It is a waiting love, a love that does not seek control.[3]

When we show up for doctors appointments, tests, treatments or surgery, there is a real sense in which we are handing ourselves over. We are letting go of being in charge of our bodies, our health and sometimes even our lives.

I struggled with this. We all struggle with this. Not only with the passivity which it seems to require, but also with the trust it requires, and most of all, with the physical surrender which it requires.

A friend and I were talking about this one day. I told her that I knew my job was to keep showing up wherever and whenever I was told to show up. "That's it," she said. "Your job is to show up. That is the most important thing you can do right now. Just show up."

This same friend had shared with me her story of showing up every day for a year to take her chemotherapy when she was fighting breast cancer. She took her chemotherapy in pill form at home. Within an hour of swallowing the pill she would become sick. In order to stay faithful to this kind of difficult showing up she put a note on her refrigerator, which read, "Chemotherapy is a gift from God." Every day she read this note, and it helped her find the strength to show up and take her medication. It was a daily practice of handing herself over. Today, some twenty-seven years later, I bless her for taking care of herself in this way. She is still blessing my life and many other peoples' lives with her presence.

Long before I was diagnosed with cancer, I had learned something about showing up when I pushed myself week after week to show up for counseling. The fear and shame that developed in me as a result of childhood trauma had followed me into adulthood. I knew I had to find a way to heal from all that trauma, but the healing required that I show up every day to journal and to pray through the pain. And it required that I show up to acknowledge my struggles in therapy. The only way I could do this was to pray daily for the humility and courage I needed to show up in these ways.

It was persistence in showing up—and God's persistence in showing up on my behalf—which were in large part responsible for the freedom I eventually came to enjoy. Perhaps the greatest surprise when we show up is the way God meets us in those difficult moments.

May you be granted the courage and humility to show up today. And may you experience God's persistence in showing up on your behalf.

When you don't know what to do…show up.

Questions for reflection and discussion

1. What experiences have you had with needing to show up?

2. What gives you the strength to show up and to keep showing up?

3. What has your experience been of God showing up for you in these difficult times?

Learn Vulnerability

Learn Vulnerability

I will remove from them their hearts of stone
and give them a heart of flesh.
Ezekiel 11:19

When I was diagnosed with cancer I felt fear, but I was not clear about what frightened me. So I prayed for clarity: "God, I know that I am afraid. But what am I most afraid of? Please show me."

Vulnerability was the word that came as a response to this prayer. Being vulnerable was what frightened me the most.

To be vulnerable is to be undefended. No fortress walls around our hearts. No live ammunition to fire in self defense. When we are vulnerable we are open to being hurt.

As the text from Ezekiel suggests, God offers to remove our hearts of stone and to give us hearts of flesh. God offers to remove the hardness of our hearts. In place of our hard hearts, God offers to give us hearts that are vulnerable—hearts that can feel both pain and joy, hearts that are tender like God's own heart.

God had been teaching me for years about vulnerability, showing me that my well-defended, stone heart kept me at a safe distance from others. It created barriers to the genuine expression of love and affection. My stone heart hindered me from receiving God's love and the love of others, and it kept me from freely offering loving affection to God and to others.

Almost all of us have wounded hearts. Many of us have had our longing for love and our longing to love others rejected in some way. As a result, most of us have some part of our heart that is defended, hardened. Like stone. We defend and protect ourselves—often without even knowing we are doing so. To the extent that we protect and defend ourselves, we hurt people close to us, causing them to feel bereft of us and in greater need of defending their own hearts.

God had been reminding me that vulnerability is the soil in which all good things grow. Love, connection, intimacy, trust, healing, kindness, honesty, genuineness all grow in the rich soil of our vulnerability.

When I prayed to know my greatest fear and *vulnerability* came back as the answer, I saw once again what I had seen through all the earlier times of crisis and struggle in my life. It was this: *the thing I was the most afraid of is the biggest gift of all.*

As I told clients, friends and family about being diagnosed with breast cancer, I prayed that I would stay in a place of vulnerability. As a result, some very open-hearted exchanges took place. There were many tears and hugs and expressions of love and affection. The most important realities in the universe are given life in the rich soil of our vulnerability.

The author of the letter to the Philippians invites us to take on the same mind set—the same way of being in the world—that Christ had. In the second chapter of this letter we read about Jesus becoming completely vulnerable. He "who being in very nature God, did not consider equality with God something to be grasped, but... taking the very nature of a servant...he humbled himself and became obedient to death—even death on a cross." (Philippians 2:5-8)

Vulnerability is at the very center of Jesus' life and death. We talk about Jesus saving us, but what do we mean when we say these familiar words? I believe that one of the ways the cross of Christ offers us salvation is that the cross shows us the way of vulnerability. Christ's death offers us salvation from our hardened hearts and defensive ways (the very things that lead us to harm others and to push God away). The cross invites us, and God's Spirit empowers us, to lay our armor down and to practice the way of vulnerability.

Margaret Bullitt-Jonas writes in her book *Christ's Passion, Our Passions* about the final words that Jesus spoke from the cross. About his words, "I thirst," she writes,

> "I thirst for you," says God. "I long for you. Will you turn to me? Will you say yes?"
>
> God is so vulnerable sometimes. We're all vulnerable when we ask for love, since love can't be forced—it can only be freely given. And never is God's longing so straightforward, so direct, as when we see God on the cross, pouring out God's self for our sake. [4]

So what exactly is vulnerability? What does it look like and feel like? It is what Margaret Bullit-Jonas is describing as she talks about God's vulnerability in Christ on the cross. Vulnerability is the full exposure of our love and our longing to be loved. It is the open expression of our spirit's deepest truth. We were made for intimate, tender relationship with God and with each other. This is our heart's deepest need and longing.

When I was a young nurse, I worked with many men and women who were in their final days of life. Some were young. Some had lived long and full lives. Many of them talked to me about their experience of coming to the end of life. From their vantage point they shared what they could now see. It was as if they had climbed a high mountain and now had a clear view of things. "It is all about loving and being loved," they told me.

This is what Jesus taught—not only in his death, but in his life as well. When people came and asked Jesus what mattered most in life, he answered simply and directly, "Love God and love your neighbor as yourself" (Matthew 22:37,38).

For me, vulnerability, comes down to allowing myself to feel and express my love and affection to God and to others with an open heart, with wisdom and with humility.

Even though vulnerability means that we don't allow our fears and defenses to rule our lives, vulnerability does *not* mean that we have no boundaries. Boundaries are very much a part of vulnerability. Boundaries are tools that allow us to respectfully, honestly and humbly communicate about our limits. Our "yes" means yes and our "no" means no. We do not feel compelled to share everything with everyone. We do not feel compelled to rescue others or to do things that are beyond our capability or power. Instead we seek God's wisdom about what we share and about how we respond to the needs of others.

Part of living with hearts of flesh—hearts that are tender and vulnerable—is that we practice honesty and respectfulness. We do not become superheros. Quite the opposite. We become children, God's much loved children—open, loving, responsive and aware of our limits.

When I let myself stay open to the experience of vulnerability during my season of living with cancer, it sometimes felt like everything inside of me was turning to liquid. It was as if I had been hard like ice in places and now I was melting. I was losing the sense of protection and definition that the hardness had offered.

This was a strange and powerful sensation that I wanted to resist. It felt like I was losing myself. It was painful. At least, it was painful as long as I resisted it. But when I let myself stay with this sensation of melting and flowing, and allowed myself to relax into it, it became something wonderful. As I allowed myself to melt and flow, I had a sense that I was flowing into the vastness of God, and that God was flowing into me.

A year or more before being diagnosed with cancer, as part of this ongoing conversation with God about the gift of vulnerability, I had written this prayer:

> You, God,
> are the vulnerable one.
> I am creature, child,

yet my heart is rock hard in places.
While your heart—
your heart is liquid love and longing.
You hold nothing back.

May God prepare us to give up our stone hearts and to receive the gift of vulnerability. May God grant us the grace to be like God in Christ, whose heart is liquid love and longing, poured out to us all.

When you don't know what to do…learn vulnerability.

Questions for reflection and discussion

1. What thoughts and feelings do you have about the idea of becoming more vulnerable?

2. What negative experiences have you had with being vulnerable?

3. What experiences have you had with vulnerability being the soil in which intimacy and love can grow?

Make Amends

Make Amends

Therefore, if you are offering your gift
at the altar and there remember that
your brother has something against you,
leave your gift there in front of the altar.
First go and be reconciled to your brother,
then come and offer your gift.
Matthew 5:23

Throughout my experience with cancer I often prayed to be given the grace to be vulnerable. Sometimes I was granted this gift, but sometimes—I think primarily when anxieties of one kind or another set in—I moved back into my defenses. Often without even knowing it.

My defenses hurt people. At a minimum, my defenses create a sense of separation from other people. As a result, others will feel held at arms length or even pushed away.

When we harm others, we have a choice to make. We can deny or minimize the harm we have caused—and thus cause more harm. We can sink into shame about how bad we are—and thus keep the focus on us while continuing to miss the needs of those we have hurt. Or we can make amends.

Making amends means that we face the truth about the harm we have done, intentional or not. It means we go to those we have harmed and acknowledge that we have hurt them, and we let them say whatever they need to say. (We only do this, however, when we are reasonably certain that doing so will not cause additional harm.)

And then, when we have acknowledged the harm we have done, we offer to do what we can to make repairs and listen carefully. We do not ask for forgiveness. We do not ask for anything from them.

Instead we offer to make things right.

Sometimes this means restoring what we have taken. Whether it is time or attention or resources. Sometimes it means praying for the grace to make changes in the way we conduct ourselves.

The gospel of Luke (19:1-9) tells the story of a man named Zacchaeus who lived in Jericho and was a tax collector. Zacchaeus heard that Jesus was passing through his town and wanted to see him. There was a large crowd and, because Zacchaeus was a small man, he was not able to see Jesus. So, in order to get a good view, Zacchaeus ran ahead of Jesus and the crowd and climbed a tree next to the road.

Tax collectors in Israel were people who by definition harmed others. They were Jewish people who were serving the Roman government by collecting taxes from their own people. They were seen as traitors. To make matters worse, their pay came from taking whatever extra they could—over and above what the Roman rulers demanded. They often took a lot for themselves. Zacchaeus evidently was making a very good living as a chief tax collector because he was a wealthy man.

When Jesus passed by the tree where Zacchaeus was waiting, he stopped and called to him, inviting himself to Zacchaeus' house. Zacchaeus, who was shunned and hated by everyone, responded to this attention. The crowd, however, was not at all pleased. They judged Jesus and said, "He has gone to be the guest of a sinner."

Luke's gospel tells us that something happened to Zacchaeus during this encounter with Jesus. Zacchaeus became willing to make amends. He is recorded as saying: "Look, Lord! Here and now I give half of my possessions to the poor, and if I have cheated anybody out of anything, I will pay back four times the amount."

That is what it means to make amends. We see that we have done harm and our desire, by God's grace, is now to repair the harm we have caused.

Not all amends can be as concrete as the amends Zacchaeus made. It is often not a matter of returning money we have taken. Sometimes the harm we have done comes from the defensive ways we have interacted with others. This kind of harm requires what some call "living amends." That is, it requires that we commit ourselves to live differently.

For me, making amends often involves praying for the humility and courage to let go of my defenses and to live from a more honest and vulnerable place. A few days before my second surgery, one of my friends left a voice message telling me that she was struggling because I had seemed defensive when she had asked how I was feeling in anticipation of the coming surgery. My defensive response had left her feeling pushed away and hurt. I made amends by calling her back and acknowledging that I had been defensive and that my defensiveness had been hurtful to her. I also told her that I did not want any walls between us. These amends and the conversation that followed helped to restore the trust between us.

We cannot live in this world without hurting others. Knowingly and unknowingly we too often break the bridge of love that keeps us connected to others. When we realize that we have done this, it is time to repair the bridge.

According to Jesus (Matthew 5:23), if we realize that we have hurt someone, making amends to them is a priority more important than worship. To make amends is to live humbly, honestly, lovingly with others. It changes us. It heals our relationships.

When you don't know what to do...make amends.

Questions for reflection and discussion

1. What have you done (or not done) during this time of difficulty that may have hurt someone else?

2. What might you do to make amends?

Stay Present in
Times of Waiting

Stay Present
In the Times
of Waiting

I wait for the Lord, my soul waits,
and in his word I put my hope.
My soul waits for the Lord
more than watchmen wait for the morning,
more than the watchmen wait for the morning.
Psalm 130: 5,6

The grocery store where I do much of our shopping has a policy to keep their check out lines no longer than three customers at a time. As soon as any of the lines get longer than this, they call for another checker.

I appreciate this. I do not like to wait. Who does? We have better things to do. I tend to think of waiting as a waste of time. It is an annoyance. A negative. Something to be avoided.

We tend to forget that waiting can be a thing of beauty. A gift. Even a blessing.

Sometimes we allow ourselves the luxury of waiting to watch a sunset so we can soak in the beauty. Or we give ourselves to prayerful waiting for a loved one to come through surgery. Or to the joyful waiting—for nine miraculous months—while a child forms in the womb. These times of waiting remind us that staying in a place of quiet anticipation does something to us. Something sacred can happen as we wait.

Waiting does not need to be a vacant, passive or negative experience. The meaning of the word is not disengagement. Quite the opposite. Waiting means an active anticipation. To wait is to watch. Like a night watchman waits and watches for the first signs of dawn. Like an expectant mother waits to meet the child she carries.

When we wait in the midst of life's difficulties, however, we often find ourselves living in anticipation not of blessing, but in anticipation of additional suffering. For this reason, we sometimes find it painful to stay present in times of waiting. We want to go numb. We want to avoid, distract, think of something else, pretend this is not happening or even do what we can to hurry things up.

Sometimes there is no way to hurry things up. Sometimes we just have to wait.

I waited ten days for my biopsy. Then I waited six days for the results. I waited five days after the results to see the surgeon. Then I waited two weeks to have an MRI done. And three days to get those results. And then I waited five weeks for surgery. After surgery I waited two weeks for complete results. And then I waited four more weeks for the second surgery. There were a few events but the experience was mostly about waiting.

I realized two things as I waited. First, each new season of waiting is connected to earlier times of waiting. One of my first experiences of waiting was waiting for biopsy results. That season of waiting ended in hearing bad news—I had breast cancer. Each time I waited for additional results my mind and body prepared for the next shock, the next bad news. This did not lead to hopeful waiting. It lead to feelings of anxiety and a tendency to go numb.

There was a very real possibility that each season of waiting with cancer might lead to more bad news about my condition. I needed to acknowledge that these fears were grounded in reality.

The second thing I saw was that the call to wait in Scripture is often paired with a call to hope in God. Scripture invited me to wait and watch for God to show up. My focus could be on waiting to see how God would provide, help and bless.

In order to stay present in the wilderness of waiting, I needed to remember that I was not only waiting for the next difficult event or the next piece of news, but I was also waiting for the grace and help in which the good news or the bad news would be wrapped.

I had experienced seasons of waiting in the past as I worked toward personal healing from childhood trauma. After the first startling, terrible memory surfaced one New Year's Eve, I prayed desperately for help and understanding. As I did so, I heard the words, "I will walk with you through this."

That became the pattern. First came the bad news of new memories and revelations—most often while in prayer. And this was followed by more prayer and waiting for some kind of help or strength or grace to come. And it did. Sometimes quickly. Sometimes slowly. The sun always, eventually rose. Grace and help always came.

These past seasons of waiting in the dark—uncertain and afraid—provided a history I could now draw upon. As I waited, this time with a diagnosis of breast cancer, I found myself wanting to be present in the waiting. I came to see, as I waited day after day, that I was not only waiting for the next event or piece of news. I was not even primarily waiting to see how God would show up at those moments in the future. Something more was happening. I was waiting for God to pour out the grace and strength I needed each day as I waited. I was waiting, watching, anticipating, opening myself up to God's presence each day that I waited.

Sometimes as I waited, I would picture myself in a desert. The image was of a vast, empty desert at night. It was dark and cold. I sat by a small campfire in this image. I was still and quiet. My ears straining for the smallest sound. My eyes searching the sky and the surrounding spaces for signs of God's presence. As I waited in this way, every day of waiting became its own gift. Some days I could feel my great thirst for God. Other days I felt joyful anticipation. And from time to time I felt God's presence so tangibly that my watching for God turned to resting with God.

Something happens to us in this kind of waiting. We are brought to attention. Our hearts and minds and spirits focus on what matters most, on what is most real, on our deepest longings for God.

When we wait as if we are watching for our soul's true love to appear, we find that the focus of our waiting is not so much about the future as it is about this present moment. This moment we can be right here, right now with our need, with our hunger, with our thirst for the One who is our Home, our Hope, our Help.

In her book *When the Heart Waits*, Sue Monk Kidd describes the gifts that can come to us in waiting:

> The fullness of one's soul evolves slowly. We're asked to go within to gestate the newness God is trying to form; we're asked to collaborate with grace.
>
> That doesn't mean that grace isn't a gift. Nor does it mean that the deliberate process of waiting produces grace. But waiting does provide the time and space necessary for grace to happen. Spirit needs a container to pour itself into. Grace needs an arena in which to incarnate. Waiting can be such a place, if we allow it.[5]

As we wait and watch in anticipation of the One-who-is-with-us to be revealed, a great work takes place within. A deeper container is carved in our souls—a container that will be able to receive more of God's life, more of God's love and grace.

It is as if the womb of our soul is enlarged as we wait in times of distress. We can stay present in our times of waiting, as a mother waits in quiet wonder. Waiting in anticipation that grace will meet us, trusting that grace is with us now. Moment by moment, day after day. One moment, one day at a time.

When you don't know what to do…stay present in times of waiting.

Questions for reflection and discussion

1. What experiences have you had with waiting in times of distress?

2. What anxieties did you feel?

3. What strength and grace did you experience?

Be Still and Keep Moving

Be Still and Keep Moving

Even youths grow tired and weary,
and young men stumble and fall;
but those that hope in the Lord
will renew their strength.
They will soar on wings like eagles,
they will run and not grow weary,
they will walk and not faint.
Isaiah 40:31

When I was told that I had cancer, my body responded. It got ready. It geared up. And not just on the day I received the diagnosis, but every day for months my body was geared up to fight for survival.

Whenever we are faced with difficulties of any kind we experience extra doses of adrenaline pulsing through our bodies. We are on alert. We are all charged up. This extra adrenaline often leaves us feeling anxious and wired.

Small amounts of adrenaline help us learn, help keep us focused on a task, and even help us do well through surgeries. But too much adrenaline makes it difficult to learn or focus on anything. And it wears us out.

So the question is, what do we do about all this extra adrenaline? How do we take care of ourselves when we are under stress?
There are two things that seem to help me the most. First, it helps me to be still every day for a period of time. And second, it helps me to keep moving. It helps me to get outside and walk, to go to the gym for a workout, to run around and play outside with our grandson.

Sit still and keep moving. We need to practice both of these things. They are helpful during times of low stress, and crucial to our functioning during times when stress is high.

When we become still and quiet, our bodies begin to calm down. The sense of threat begins to lessen. When we couple this with intentionally slowing down our breathing, we can reduce the amount of adrenaline being pumped into our blood stream and when we get moving we can metabolize some of the extra adrenaline. The adrenaline is there to help us fight or run faster than we normally could. Our bodies are ready to move and moving helps to use up extra adrenaline.

Normally I go to the gym three times a week and work out for an hour. But a few days after I was diagnosed with cancer, I realized that I needed to walk on the days that I was not at the gym. At least, as often as possible. And I did. It gave me extra time alone to pray. It got me outside more. It gave me a sense of being partially in charge of my body. It felt like a gift I was giving myself.

Normally I spend time nearly every day in quiet. Reading, journaling, praying, meditating. This also needed to be increased. I had more going on to journal about—more feelings, more inventory, more prayers. I could feel my need for quiet stillness. I hungered for more time alone in quiet with God. So I allowed myself more time whenever possible. This, too, was a gift I gave myself.

It might be helpful to brainstorm ways that you enjoy being still and ways you enjoy being active. Consider posting these two lists somewhere so you can refer to them easily during times when you are too tired or too agitated to remember them.

A list of quiet activities might include listening to calming music, soaking in the bath, breathing slowly and easily for several minutes, meditating, reading, praying, or simply being still and quiet. A list of moving activities could include walking, biking, hiking, gardening, going for a run, dancing, going to the gym.

It is clear that both being still and being active take time. This means that taking care of ourselves in these ways will need to become a priority. This is often not an easy thing for us to do. We often live our lives responding to other people's needs and being unaware of our own. But it is always a gift—not only to ourselves but to everyone in our lives—when we take good care of ourselves. In fact, when we don't take care of ourselves we are not really able to care well for others. So we need to be willing to say no to some of the demands in our lives (including our own demands of ourselves) in order to find time to be still and to keep moving.

Take good care of you. You are God's beloved child. You are of infinite value. Find time to be still and time to move.

When you don't know what to do…be still and keep moving.

Questions for reflection and discussion

1. What are your favorite ways to rest and relax?

2. What are your favorite ways to be active?

3. What are you doing to take care of yourself during this difficult time?

Know You Are Not Alone

Know You Are
Not Alone

I am with you always.
Matthew 28:20

There was a very real sense in which breast cancer was not something that was just happening to me. It was happening to everyone in my life. But there was also a very real sense in which it was only happening to me. No one else was going through exactly what I was going through. Our suffering is always uniquely ours.

I was the one who was facing surgery. I was the one who had to show up at all the appointments with doctors. I was the one who had to keep paying attention to this threat. I was the one who was experiencing this the most directly. No one else was fully in this with me.

This felt lonely at times.

I think that the most lonely thing of all was not being able to fully share the emotional and spiritual experiences I was going through with people close to me. What I was experiencing was never simple. It was always complex, multi-layered, textured. If I tried to explain one aspect of my experience to my friends, they would hear what I was saying, but it felt like a loss to me that I was not able to also put into words the five other things that were going on at the same time.

And when I started to share the spiritual gifts that graced my days—the sense of God's tender presence, the moments of clarity when it felt I had stepped into heaven on earth—I couldn't speak. Words failed me.

Besides, here were my friends worrying about me—and here I was—experiencing not only fear and distress but moments of joy and blessedness. I was afraid they would not be able to see what I longed to show them because of their concerns for me and because I had no way to even sketch the edges of these holy moments.

There were times, however, of holding hands with my husband across a table at a restaurant and sharing an experience or reflection from the day, when he would listen attentively and his eyes would brim with tears of deep knowing and understanding. Those moments were moments of oneness, of union, of quiet joy. He heard me with an open heart and understood. Such moments made me treasure him even more deeply. And such moments helped me feel less alone.

There were also times of sharing with women who were breast cancer survivors that involved a spirit-to-spirit connection. One woman in particular who is the wife of one of my husband's colleagues, but whom I had only met once, emailed me briefly about her own experience. She had recently gone through surgery and chemotherapy for breast cancer. Part of what she put words to was the deep spiritual experience she had. I knew she knew. She gave voice to some of what seemed beyond words to me at the time.

Difficult life experiences have a way of creating a deeper sacred space within us, a greater opening in our spirits to receive the most remarkable truth of all: we are not alone. We have never been alone. God is always with us.

The bare fact of this truth was not new for me. I had experienced this as I walked through the healing of childhood sexual abuse years earlier. It was a painful and lonely journey. I had the support and love of others throughout this entire journey. I could not have done it without them, but they could not enter the darkest of places inside. They could not feel the full weight of my shame, my fear or my despair.

But there is One who could. God's Spirit was with me. As Comforter. As Friend. As Healer. As the Presence of tender, intimate love.

When I was early in the journey of recovery from childhood abuse, the wounded child in me wanted nothing to do with the thought that God was with me when I was experiencing abuse. This thought created complete confusion for me. How was it possible, for God to have been there with me and to not have stopped what was happening? My child's mind shuttered at this thought.

It took a long time for me to be ready to invite God to show me how God was with me in that darkness, but I was eventually able to do this. The first vision I had after inviting God to open my eyes was a vision of a room in which I was being abused as a child. The abuse was taking place. I had seen this event before many times. But this time the room was transformed. It was filled with light, God's own light and the light of angels too many for my young mind to count. I was stunned, breathless.

Several weeks later I saw another vision. Again I was being hurt in a room in this same house. And, again, I had visited this scene several times. When I invited God to show me how God was present at that time, I saw Jesus kneeling on one knee next to where I was on the floor. But some little kid part of me was also wrapped in Jesus' arms. Jesus' jaw was tight with distress, his presence was strong and tender. A part of me was held. In the middle of the worst kind of suffering, I was held. I was loved.

Over several years, memory after memory of abuse came. And vision after vision of Jesus with me, loving me, holding me, came as well. The horror and the powerful, tender love. I thought that in those terrible times I had been forgotten, abandoned. But I was never alone.

Somehow God was not only with me but my pain and suffering were somehow God's own pain and suffering. God suffers all things with us. God shares all sorrow and all joy with us. So when

I poured my heart out to God about all that I was feeling and experiencing, I came to understand that God knew. In fact, God knew more than I knew about the depths of my suffering—long before I was able to acknowledge it.

Revisiting the pain of childhood abuse is a painful process, but the gains and gifts that came to me are beyond measure. I know now that deep in the heart of our suffering, in the darkest and most painful corners of memory, God is at work. Long before we are able to begin the healing journey, God has been at work preparing the way for us. God is with each of us. Absolutely. Always. And God fully knows with complete empathy and compassion what we are experiencing, even those experiences that are beyond words.

Some mornings when I am out walking I look up at the sky and it seems far away. On other days I realize that the sky kisses the earth. As I walk, I move through sky. I walk surrounded by sky. I breath in the sky. It lives inside of me.

Whether the sky seems close or far away, the truth is that it is always close.

And, so it is with God. God is the One in whom we "live and breathe and have our being" (Acts 17:28). God is with us. Always. God's loving presence caresses us, surrounds us, fills us.

I am not alone. You are not alone. God is with us. And God knows. You can trust this absolutely.

When you don't know what to do…know you are not alone.

Questions for reflection and discussion

1 What experiences have you had of feeling alone during difficult times?

2. What has helped you feel less alone?

3. What experiences have you had of God's presence with you?

Ask For Healing

Ask for Healing

Praise the Lord, O my soul;
all my inmost being, praise his holy name.
Praise the Lord, O my soul,
and forget not all his benefits
who forgives all your sins
and heals all your diseases,
who redeems your life from the pit
and crowns you with love and compassion,
who satisfies your desires with good things
so that your youth is renewed like the eagle's.
Psalm 103:1-5

When we think about praying for healing some of us may envision a television evangelist shouting and making demands of God to heal people who are crowded in front of a stage with their crutches and wheelchairs. All of this may seem too pressured, too staged and too centered on the faith healer.

It is also true that when we think about asking for healing, we may find ourselves remembering times in the past when we felt shame for what we experienced as a lack of faith because we weren't quite able to "name and claim" our healing. We may feel that we don't have enough faith to pray in this way.

Such images and fears create barriers which prevent us from talking to God about our need for physical, emotional and spiritual healing. But we do not need to let ourselves be robbed in this way. We can come to God, as children might go to a loving parent, and ask for our heart's desire.

I did this. I asked God to heal my cancer.

I did not do this right away. But one day, while sitting quietly in prayer, I asked God to show me how to pray about my cancer.

As I waited I had an image come to mind of the cancer cells melting and being carried out of my body. So I put my hand on the biopsy site and prayed that God would melt the cancer cells and allow them to be carried out of my body. I then "watched" as they disintegrated and were carried away.

The moments of praying in this way were not accompanied by feelings of certainty that my prayer would be answered. Nor did I feel like I needed to generate such feelings. Instead these moments felt like child-like asking. I felt comforted simply by asking God to heal me.

I make no claim to a great miracle, but I was deeply grateful when I was told that the cancer which the surgeon removed was very small in size. It was so small, in fact that I only needed to have a small amount of tissue removed and no need for the normal seven weeks of radiation therapy. I took this news as pure grace. I wondered if God had melted the cancer cells and washed them away, leaving only enough for the surgeon to know that she had found what she was looking for.

The important thing for me in all of this was to ask. Asking God to show me how to pray and then inviting God to touch my body in this way gave me a greater sense of intimacy with God. I invited God, my Healer, God my Surgeon, God my Creator to lovingly touch my body. In doing so, I experienced God gently touching my heart and my soul as well.

I asked God to show me how to pray about my physical health during the months of living with cancer. The way I most often pray for emotional and spiritual healing also comes out of what I sense God has been teaching me. I pray that God will heal and release me (and others) from fear, shame, pride, greed, self-serving and defensiveness. I also pray that God will free me to live in a place of trust and hope and humility. And I pray that God will free me to receive all of God's good gifts to me each day, especially the gift of awareness of God's Presence.

The answers to these prayers for emotional and spiritual healing come slowly. But they do come. Over the years I have seen deep and significant changes in my own life and in the lives of others. I think this kind of healing is slow primarily because true and lasting change always takes time. A little at a time we are released from fear, shame, pride, greed, self-reliance and defensiveness. A little at a time we are freed to take in God's love and to allow that love to fill us and flow out to others.

I have experienced God's Spirit to be a gentle and persistent healer of our hearts and minds. Our work is to be faithful in seeking this healing, in staying as open as possible to this grace. And, so I pray day after day, year after year for healing for myself, for those I know and for all people everywhere.

Psalm 103 reminds us that God is the One who "satisfies our desires with good things." I had not always trusted that God was good and kind and intimately loving. For years I privately feared that God was distant and disapproving and uninterested in my needs and feelings. But over time, as I have asked for increased awareness of God's love, my eyes and heart have opened more and more, allowing me to see and receive more fully the reality of God's intimate, tender love for me and for us all.

When I pray for healing or help of any kind I do not focus on how much faith I have or how much I believe. I focus instead on God. I pray with the awareness that God is love. That God is always with us. That God's desire is always to help us, care for us and bless us. That God's intentions for us are always for good. And that God invites us to bring everything to God in prayer.

> God,
> Heal and release us
>   from our fear and shame and guilt,
>   from our pride and greed and self reliance,
>   from our guardedness and defensiveness.

Free us to be our truest child-like selves,
trusting, resting, humble, receptive, joyful, loving, loved.

Awaken us to your loving presence,
that may we receive more and more of your good gifts
to us—your love and grace and peace and joy and light
and life.

And grant us the humility and wisdom to live
in full, joyful surrender to your loving will.
May your kingdom of love and goodness come,
may your will be done in our lives this day and always.
Amen.

When you don't know what to do…ask for healing.

Questions for reflection and discussion

1. What emotional, spiritual or physical healing have you experienced during this difficult time?

2. What healing do you want to ask God about at this time?

Seek Guidance

Seek Guidance

Whether you turn to the right or the left,
your ears will hear a voice behind you, saying,
"This is the way, walk in it."
Isaiah 30:21

The day after Christmas my husband and I met for the first time with the surgeon. She was the one who would tell me what I needed to have done and what losses I would encounter in the process of treatment.

She told us a great many things that morning—more than I could absorb. The bottom line was that the treatment I needed was not yet clear. The path was uncertain.

To begin with, the surgeon ordered an MRI to get as much information as possible before making a plan. This meant a wait. First for approval of the MRI from my medical insurance provider. Then waiting to schedule the MRI. And, finally, it meant waiting for the results of the MRI.

We walked out of the surgeon's office that morning without a treatment plan. We knew there were two basic possibilities for this kind of breast cancer. I might be fortunate enough to have a lumpectomy followed by weeks of daily radiation therapy, or I might need to have a mastectomy. The path ahead was not clear.

When we are afraid and the path ahead is unclear, we tend to want to take control. I certainly do. It is not easy to tolerate not knowing.

There are lots of things we can do when the path ahead is unclear. Sometimes collecting more information is helpful. So I started to gather information.

I looked at all the information I could find on the two possible options. And even though I did not know which option I would need to take in the end, I mentally and emotionally "tried on" these two possibilities. I knew that I was trying to prepare myself for what was ahead, even though I did not know what that might be.

It took a while, but I eventually realized that I needed to stop reading about lumpectomies, radiation, mastectomies and reconstruction. The plain truth was that I did not know what was ahead of me. I had more information than I knew what to do with. And the information I really needed, about my specific situation and options, was not yet available. I needed to stay in the place of not knowing.

Elizabeth Gilbert, in her book, *Eat, Pray, Love*, writes about her very first experience of prayer. She was in a time of great crisis, crying on the floor of her bathroom in the dark hours of the early morning. She found herself praying, "I am in desperate need of help. I don't know what to do. I need an answer. Please tell me what to do. Please tell me what to do. Please tell me what to do." After she stopped crying, she found herself in a place of silence. This is how she describes her experience:

> I was surrounded by something I can only describe as a little pocket of silence—a silence so rare that I didn't want to exhale, for fear of scaring it off. I was seamlessly still. I don't know when I'd ever felt such stillness. Then I heard a voice....How can I describe the warmth of affection in that voice, as it gave me the answer that would forever seal my faith in the divine. The voice said: Go back to bed, Liz. I exhaled. It was so immediately clear that this was the only thing to do...True wisdom gives the only possible answer at any given moment, and that night, going back to bed was the only possible answer. Go back to bed, said this omniscient interior voice, because the only thing you need to do for now is get some rest and take good care of yourself until you do know the answer.[6]

I had learned in my years recovering from childhood trauma that I was usually given only enough light on the path to see the next step. My job was to simply take that next step, without knowing where all this was going.

So, as I sought guidance about my cancer, I knew the drill. Stay in the dark. Stay right where I was. Be still. Be silent. Pray for guidance. Know that the guidance I needed would come, and, as Elizabeth puts it, "get some rest and take good care of myself until the time when I knew the answer."

Something the surgeon told us at that first consultation, the day after Christmas, stuck with me. She had told us that some women with this diagnosis opt for double mastectomies and breast implants. I remember being stunned when she said this. It didn't make sense to me at the time. This breast cancer that I had was not life threatening. It was contained. But some women had double mastectomies with this kind of breast cancer?

A few days after hearing this story, I found myself reflecting on what the surgeon had told us about why a woman would do this. She had explained that some women make this choice, when all they might need is a lumpectomy and radiation, because they do not want to ever have to face this particular threat again. They don't ever want to be told that they have breast cancer again. They don't ever want to wait for results from a mammogram again. They want to take charge.

I understood this. I wanted to take charge in some way. I sympathized with these women who made such a radical choice. But I knew that for me, such a choice would be based in fear. And I did not want to let fear guide me.

Seeking guidance from God when the way is unclear is not an easy thing for me. It is something I try to practice in all kinds of circumstances, but it is not always easy. It means waiting. It means living with not knowing. It means not being in charge. It means trusting. It means surrender.

After all the testing and waiting was complete, the surgeon's best advice was to start by doing a lumpectomy, wait for the results and then see where to go from there. I struggled with following this advice because the surgeon had told me the story of a patient who had gone back into surgery four times, trying to get clean margins all the way around the cancer, only to have to finally give up and have a mastectomy. This did not sound easy to me.

The other thing I wrestled with was that a mastectomy would offer a one percent chance of reoccurrence, whereas a lumpectomy with radiation would leave a five to six percent chance of reoccurrence. That difference may seem rather small, but I now knew what it was like to be told there was a ninety percent chance that I did not have cancer, only to find out that I did have cancer. Every percent seemed big to me.

I weighed all this. And prayed. And talked. And prayed. And sat in silence, listening.

In the end it seemed wise to follow the doctor's advice. Have a lumpectomy. Take one small step even if there might be several more steps to follow. Don't get out in front of the advice I was being given.

There was no brick from heaven with a note attached. There was no thunder. The sense of being guided was quiet, subdued even. Like a whisper in my ear, "This is the way, walk in it."

I told my husband what I was thinking and asked for his input. "I think you are making a good decision," he said thoughtfully, "you are following the doctors best advice, and that seems wise."

I never dreamt that the outcome in my case would be so positive. I never imagined that the amount of cancer would be so tiny that I would be told that I did not need radiation. I never thought that I would come out of this so unscathed, cancer free, being told I had only a very small chance of reoccurrence. But I did.

I am grateful that I did not second guess the doctor or run ahead of God's guidance out of fear. I am grateful that I was given the grace to take one step at a time into the unknown.

Scripture tells us, "When any of you lacks wisdom, he should ask God, who gives generously to all without finding fault, and it will be given to him." (James 1:5) We often do not know the way. But God does. And God offers to give us the wisdom we need, and promises to give it generously. One step at a time.

When you don't know what to do…seek guidance.

Questions for reflection and discussion

1. What guidance have you sensed from God in this time of difficulty?

2. What guidance do you need right now?

Meditate

Meditate

May the words of my mouth
and the meditations of my heart
be pleasing in your sight,
O Lord, my Rock and my Redeemer.
Psalm 19:14

Many of us have times when we our minds race. Our minds might randomly switch from one thought to another. Or repeatedly rehearse a future event. Or play a past event over and over. Sometimes our minds get fixed on one idea and miss everything else. Or our minds try to figure things out—as if by thinking hard enough we can make sense out of things that make no sense.

All of these mental gymnastics can keep us distracted and agitated. Very little of this mental activity is productive. In fact, it is often quite destructive. Whether we are playing out some future fantasy or disaster or getting lost in some mental maze, it usually increases our distress.

What we need in times like this is to bring our minds back to the present moment. We need to slow down our racing thoughts and experience the here and now.

Meditation is a spiritual practice which can help us do this. Meditation pulls us out of our spinning, obsessing minds, into our hearts, and from our hearts, eventually, into the sacred core of our being where our spirits know themselves to be held safe by the loving Spirit of God.

Most religious traditions encourage some kind of meditative practice and offer some kind of instruction on the various ways to practice meditation. Most of these approaches to meditation have a few basic elements in common.

Most meditative practices involve sitting still for a period of time. They also involve attending to our breathing as a simple way of quieting our minds and allowing us to bring ourselves back to our bodies here and now in this moment. And most meditative practices involve some kind of focal point—a word or a phrase or an image to sit with—to absorb or to be absorbed into.

This quietness and stillness of body and mind puts us in a listening mode. We quiet our internal and external voice and listen for the Voice of the One who made us, sustains us and loves us.

Thomas Merton, in his book, *Contemplative Prayer*, describes meditation as "an attentive, watchful listening of the heart." He goes on to say that it "begins not so much with 'considerations' as with a 'return to the heart,' finding one's deepest center, awakening the profound depths of our being in the presence of God who is the source of our being and our life." [7]

The book of Psalms talks about meditation as a normal part of life. The psalmists describe meditating on God's "unfailing love" (Psalm 48:9), on God's "precepts and promises" (Psalm 119:78,148) and on God's "wonderful works" (Psalm 145:5).

Meditation is a refocusing of our minds and hearts on a Power greater than ourselves, and that act of refocusing can have a profound impact on us—physically, emotionally, spiritually and relationally.

Meditation moves us out of our obsessing minds, out of our self-reliance, out of our endless striving. It moves us into the wonder, the beauty, the love and the truth of God. It helps us move from a place of agitation to a place where we can rest.

Meditation does not need to be complicated. We don't need to set aside many hours a day or learn some secret practice in order to meditate. We can begin simply. And we can continue simply. We might slow our breathing, come back to the present moment, and quietly, repeatedly bring our minds back to a word. I will sometimes do this, coming back to a word like "rest". Or I might focus on one of the many names for God: Light. Peace. Comfort. Beautiful One. Healer. Almighty. Love. Goodness. Joy. Shepherd. Counselor. The purpose of whatever word we choose is to simply express our consent to rest in God's presence.

The practice of meditation is actually simple. What is not so simple is what goes on inside our minds as we practice meditation. Most of us find that our minds quiet for a moment or two as we sit still and focus on our breathing and then on a word or phrase. But then our minds come right back at us with all kinds of ideas and suggestions and noise.

Part of the work of meditation is to expect this, to notice when this is happening and to accept it with humility and humor. When it happens we come back to the word we have chosen, expressing again our intent to rest in God's loving presence. We need to breathe easily and refocus again. And again. And again.

Meditation can also be a guided experience. Before my cancer surgeries I listened many times to a meditation by Belleruth Naparstek.[8] It was designed to prepare a person for a successful surgery. She talks the listener through slowing their breathing and seeing themselves in a safe place with someone who loves them. As part of this meditation, she guides listeners through a process of visualizing the coming surgery. During this guided meditation I watched myself being wheeled into surgery where a loving and skillful team of professionals cared for me and where all goes exceptionally well. On several occasions these meditations led to significant spiritual encounters. On one occasion in the silence of meditation I saw myself on a deserted beach with Jesus. I felt completely safe, fully loved, filled with joy in this scene. And then, as I sat with Jesus and he reviewed with me the images of my upcoming surgery, I felt a growing ease and confidence and even gratitude about it all.

One of the most powerful things that I experienced during these guided meditations was an image of Jesus present with me in the operating room. He stood at the foot of the bed and gently placed a hand on my ankle.

It was an image I had seen previously—not in a scene about an anticipated surgery, but in a long forgotten scene of abuse from my childhood. This vision came to me several times during the years of remembering and healing from childhood trauma. Often when I would sit still, slow my breathing and invite God to show me whatever God chose to show me, I would see images of the abuse I experienced during childhood. I would sometimes see myself as a child being hurt, and all the while Jesus was there, with his hand on my ankle. Through the touch of his hand I could feel an energy unlike anything I had ever felt. It was, I concluded, the life giving energy of pure love. It would fill my heart and mind and body. Like an internal baptism, it cleansed me and strengthened me and healed me.

The experience of those moments was transformational. I came to know that God's love, as expressed in Jesus, is far greater and more powerful than all the hate and harm I had experienced. I came to know that God's love is far greater and far more powerful than all the hate and harm in the world.

I came to know that we can receive this pure, powerful love. We can be baptized with this love, we can be filled with this love.
It was love that healed me from the fear and shame I carried as a result of being hurt as a child. Love that flowed into me in many forms. Sometimes in the form of healing energy from the touch of Jesus' hand.

And now, here it was again. That touch. That life giving love-energy coming from Jesus' hand and filling me as I envisioned myself in surgery. I felt the gentleness of this love, the warm light of it, the life giving power of it again as I meditated.

Sometimes meditation, whether guided or not, leads to these kinds of sacred encounters, but sometimes meditation leads to other kinds of sacred encounters. Sometimes when I meditate, I encounter silence. There are times for me when that silence feels like a great void and I am aware of my great longing for God. Over time I have come to see that this, too, is a sacred experience. Sometimes the silence feels like the very presence of God.

We do not need to control our experience as we meditate. Rather, we can be open to accept whatever experience comes as the gift we are being given at the moment. In meditation we learn to listen to our own hearts and our own spirits, but we also open ourselves to the voice and the presence of God.

Bring your anxious, distressed mind and body into a place of quiet stillness. And let yourself be blessed.

When you don't know what to do...meditate.

Questions for reflection and discussion

1. What experiences have you had with meditation?

2. Let yourself practice meditating. Sit comfortably supported, take a few easy breaths, invite God to help you quiet your mind and body and to rest in God's presence. Choose a word that reflects some aspect of God's character and gently bring your mind back to this word each time you are distracted. Allow yourself to relax into God's love for you.

Pursue Peace

Pursue Peace

Peace I leave with you;
my peace I give to you.
John 14:25

Recieving a diagnosis of cancer left me in a state of anxiety that lasted for months. Struggling with the impact of childhood trauma had increased my anxiety for years. Just hearing or reading the daily news can sometimes leave me anxious. Life is full of anxiety.

Anxiety can lead to many kinds of problems. Sometimes we stay busy in an attempt, usually unsuccessful, to distract ourselves from our anxiety. Or we allow our anxiety to feed our irritability and reactivity. Or we get trapped in obsessive thinking. Or we try to control things which are beyond our control—like other people. Or we try to numb our uncomfortable anxious feelings with too much television or work or alcohol.

In all these ways we suffer because of anxiety. Often other people suffer as well because of our unchecked (and sometimes unacknowledged) anxiety.

How do we move out of our anxiety and fear into the peace that Jesus offers to us? What is the path?

The path to peace includes many of the practices we have already talked about. It includes staying grounded in reality, easing our breathing, surrendering ourselves and all that holds our hearts to God's loving care. It includes letting go of our defensiveness and living with a tender, vulnerable heart. And it includes practicing prayer and meditation on a regular basis. All of these things help to reduce the internal conflict we experience. These practices help our hearts and minds to focus on a single purpose—replacing our anxiety with the peaceful, loving care of God and living in that love. It is this singleness of purpose that quiets the internal wars. Another way to say this is that we surrender everything to the single purpose of living a life of love.

Peace within and peace in our relationships are connected. When the conflict within is quieted by releasing all that is beyond our control to God's loving care and by seeking God's guidance, we are far more able to extend grace in our relationships. When we are open and vulnerable with others, when we take inventory of our resentments and make amends, when we are aware of causing harm, not only do our relationships benefit from greater peacefulness but we also experience greater internal peace.

When we read in Scripture "Do not fear," or "Do not be anxious," it can feel like we are being commanded to do the impossible. But these texts are actually words of comfort. They are almost always followed by words of reassurance that we are not alone. That God is with us. The point is not that we should feel differently, but that all is well because God is with us. The Psalmist says it this way. "Even when I walk through the valley of the shadow of death, I will fear no evil, for you are with me." (Psalm 23:4)

It may seem impossible to imagine experiencing peace when we are in the shadow of death. But it is possible. It is possible in the middle of our most anxious times to walk the path towards peace and to ask for the gift of peace.

A few years ago I felt that God was asking me to do something outside my comfort zone. So I talked to God about my fear. During one of these times of prayer, it seemed that Jesus was gently speaking words of peace to me. "I give you my peace. I give you my peace."

It seemed clear at the time that my work was to receive the peace that was being offered. What I needed to do was to breathe in peace. And so, during times of prayer and meditation in the days that followed, I came back to those words: I give you peace. Sometimes I pictured Jesus standing in front of me breathing his peace into the room and into me. It became a meditation of listening and responding. I listened as Jesus spoke: "I give you my peace." And I responded: "I receive your peace." The rhythm of this kind of prayer was an important part of the experience. I exhaled as I listened to Jesus' words: "I give you my peace." I inhaled as I responded: "I receive your peace." The results of this form of prayer ritual were not immediate. But over time I felt increasingly carried by peace and filled with peace.

> Give me peace, Lord,
> not a hopeless resignation,
> giving in to the darkness,
> but a growing certainty that
> one day Light will dawn.
>
> Give me peace,
> not a deadening Novocain
> that robs outrage,
> but a quiet awareness of your Presence
> in the angst of the day.
>
> Give me peace,
> not a passionless state
> of not-seeing, not-knowing,
> but a fierce, calm clarity
> about what matters most.
>
> Give me peace,
> not a smugness or pretense,
> but an internal sense of being held
> that allows me to live as outrageously
> as one who is loved would live.

When you don't know what to do…pursue peace.

Questions for reflection and discussion

1. What anxieties are you experiencing?

2. Write your concerns on a piece of paper and put them in a box which you have designated as your "prayer box" or your "God box."

3. Sit quietly, breathe slowly, listen to Jesus say to you, "My peace I give to you." Allow yourself to breathe in the peace of God.

Acknowledge Death

Acknowledge Death

Teach us to number our days aright,
that we may gain a heart of wisdom.
Psalm 90:12

L ife is full of loss. There are little losses and big losses. Ultimately, no matter how hard we try to stave it off, death itself will come to us and to those we love.

Whenever we are faced with any difficulty, it is likely to have woven into it the fear of some kind of loss, some kind of death.

I soon realized that even though the kind of breast cancer I had was not life threatening, I was faced with a variety of little deaths. And with death itself. All of these deaths seemed to call out to be acknowledged.

Often we try to ignore the losses of life. We tend to think of death as something that happens to other people or that is very far away from us. We forget that every breath we draw, every beat of our heart is a gift given and received. We forget that we have little or no control over our life or our death and we pay a high price for our systematic inattentiveness to the many losses we experience. Our losses, while painful, are also the soil in which growth is made possible.

One of the gifts that our many losses bring to us is the possibility, as the psalmist puts it, of "gaining a heart of wisdom."

Christmas day, only a few days after first hearing the doctor explain that I had cancer, I wrote this about death:

Tomorrow I will meet with the surgeon. And the chances are

100% that she will need to take some or all of my breast. I am beginning to lose parts of my body. At times this seems a small event. And it is, in the larger perspective of things. It is a small death in a world of horrible, startling deaths. Yet it is a death. A death of being whole in body. At the same time I am experiencing a death of more and more of my pride, of more and more of my ego. Perhaps these deaths are an invitation to seek gifts from You. Gifts of humility and courage and grace and humor and openness to love. I want these gifts. I ask for all the humility and all the courage and all the grace and all the tenderhearted openness and all the humor I need for each step of this journey.

Later that day I continued with this prayer.

God, I offer you this new dying, this new death. May your life be born in this new letting go of self. Open my hands and heart and mind to release, to open up, to let go, to be emptied of pride and self-reliance and fear and self-serving. May your kingdom come and your will be done.

Nearly a month later, still waiting for what would be my first surgery, I wrote, again about death.

God. I am so sad today. I feel like I am going to die. And I am. Some day. This feels like the first of a long series of deaths. It also feels like a baptism into the absolute truth of my mortality.
It is not easy living in a body. It is at times glorious. But often it is painful. Because to fully inhabit our bodies and be here with others is to know loss upon loss.

The religious culture I was raised in mostly avoided this pain by preaching a kind of disembodied spirituality. In this way of thinking the body doesn't really matter and death is seen as a kind of inconvenience. Today I cannot abide this Gnostic defense against the reality of loss and grief. Teach me to live fully present, fully embodied, fully human. Help me to be willing to acknowledge death."

This struggle to acknowledge in a deeper, truer way that I, too, am going to die, that in many ways I am in the process of dying, brought gifts of wisdom and grace. With clearer eyes and a more tender heart I saw the exquisite beauty of the gift of life. And I caught glimpses of the gift of eternity. My sorrow began to mix with gratitude for these gifts of clearer sight. Six weeks after I was diagnosed with cancer I wrote about this gratitude.

> Thank you for this experience. Thank you that I know in a deeper way that I am mortal. Thank you for this gentle new baptism into the joyful reality of eternity. Eternity here and now, and ongoing. Eternity meaning You here with us each and all. Eternity meaning the beauty and truth and goodness of You now and always with us, in us, around us…Thank you for the surprising joy of mortality, for the hope of the bliss of seeing You one day face to face.

Death. Our instinct is to resist, to avoid, to deny. Still it is with us every day. We can keep resisting or we can give ourselves to God and ask for the strength and courage and humility to open ourselves to what seems to us to be impossibly difficult. Perhaps this openness is the ultimate vulnerability, the deepest surrender.

When you don't know what to do…acknowledge death.

Questions for reflection and discussion

1. What losses have you experienced?

2. What confrontation with death have you experienced?

3. How have these losses and confrontations impacted you?

Grieve

Grieve

Blessed are those who mourn
for they will be comforted.
Matthew 5.4

I was first introduced to the term "grief work" as a nursing student in my early twenties. I knew nothing about grief. The religious culture in which I had been raised didn't grieve much. At least not that I ever saw. Our preachers sometimes said things at funerals that would stun the average person. Things like, "This is not a day for grief, but a day for celebration." While the preacher was saying this he would usually be looking right at the grief stricken family, who would often nod in pressured agreement.

The idea that grief involved *work* fascinated me. It was as if participation in grieving was a task to be accomplished. I did know about accomplishing tasks. Tasking was something I had learned to value. So putting *grief* and *work* side by side gave me some permission to explore the idea of grief as something that actually might be important. Maybe even useful.

It turns out that grief is important. It is useful. And it is work. Grief work is vital to our health. Grieving our losses helps us maintain our mental, emotional and spiritual health.

Grief work begins when we let ourselves face a painful truth, a truth that we would rather turn away from. The truth might be that someone we love is using drugs. Or that we have hurt someone with our unkind words. Or that the abandonment we experienced in early life had a deep and long-lasting impact on us. Or that we really miss the person in our life who died. Or that we have cancer and need to have surgery.

These are painful realities. We want to look away, to numb

ourselves, to distract ourselves, to say it isn't so bad. But how will we find the healing we need if we do not pay attention to these painful truths? And what kind of people will we be if we harden our hearts to the pain in our lives and in the lives of others?

I avoided and denied and minimized the pain I carried with me from my childhood for many years. This cost me dearly. And it cost the people close to me dearly. My failure to pay attention to the work of grief meant that I wasn't real. I wasn't fully present. My heart was defended and this defensiveness left me feeling separated from myself, from God and from others. Something was missing from my closest relationships. What was missing was *me*. The most tender hearted part of me was hidden behind a wall of emotional numbness.

The *work* in grief work refers to the effort it takes to pay attention to painful truths. Even though we fear that we cannot bear it. Even though it hurts horribly. Even though we find ourselves "falling apart." The work of grief is to allow ourselves to soften and open up our hearts. It also takes work to let go. To let go of our defenses. To let go of our pride. To let go of trying to control what we cannot control.

At its heart, grief is an expression of love. If we find out we have cancer, we grieve because it turns out that no matter how flawed we may see ourselves, we love our bodies and the life they make possible. They are precious, miraculous. It also turns out that no matter how difficult life can seem at times, we love life. Life is a sweet, sweet gift. We grieve any threat to our life because we love life.

We grieve the loss of a relationship through death or separation because we love the person we have lost and the relationship we had with them or longed to have with them.

The connection between grief and love is very important. It is this connection which explains why we do not need to be afraid of our grief. It is a manifestation of our love. Grief work, then, is opening our hearts to painful realities and letting our tears flow with our tenderhearted love.

But this opening is just the beginning. Grief work is also about receiving. "Blessed are they who mourn," Jesus said, "for they will be comforted." Grief work is about allowing ourselves to receive comfort. Comfort from God. Comfort from others.

The image that comes to my mind when I think of receiving comfort is that of a child being held and loved by a safe, caring parent. The parent is attuned to the child's distress and is present to soothe, hold and support the child in compassionate love.

The Scriptures teach us that God is the "Father of all Compassion and the God of all comfort who comforts us in all our troubles" (II Corinthians 1:1-3). Giving and receiving comfort is an intimate experience. It is an emotionally close and vulnerable thing to do. To receive comfort from God is to know that God is with us, it is to let God feel our pain with us, it is to allow God to love us.

Letting God comfort us is letting God be who God is. It is letting God be the God of all comfort.

My experience is that this process of opening our hearts to painful realities, of letting go of our defenses, of releasing our tears, and of receiving comfort is a cyclic process. At first we can only open up a little, let go a little and receive a little comfort. As we do this, we are strengthened with greater courage and humility and love to open up and let go and receive more deeply. And then, again, more deeply. And again and again and again.

All of this changes us in many important ways. We become more compassionate. We grow less and less afraid of pain. We become more capable of receiving comfort and thus of experiencing ourselves as loved.

Many years ago I was grieving over childhood losses. The grief I was experiencing was more painful than I thought I could possibly tolerate. I prayed for help and comfort. As I prayed I had a sense of God inviting me to place my breaking heart in God's hand. And so, I did. My thought was that God would mend this ripped-open heart of mine. The image I saw, however, was of God gently holding my heart and breaking it all the way open.

Immediately upon seeing this image I thought of the image of Jesus breaking the loaf of bread that a small child had brought to him. There were thousands of people who had come miles to hear Jesus teach and at the end of the day they were all hungry. So Jesus asked if anyone had food. A child brought his small lunch and gave it to Jesus. Jesus took the bread and broke it open and gave it to his disciples to distribute. And all were fed.

My heart needed to be broken all the way open. God took my heart and broke through the defenses and hardness. The result was a more compassionate heart. A more tender heart. A heart capable of giving and receiving love. A heart that could be available to nourish others who were hungry for love.

Do not be afraid to grieve. It is a beautiful thing. It is a clear expression of your love. It will open you to receive more fully the love that is offered to you, and it will free you to share your love with others. And that is, after all, what life is all about.

When you don't know what to do…grieve.

Questions for reflection and discussion

1. What grief work are you doing or needing to do?

2. What support do you need as you grieve?

3. How do you see your grief as an expression of your love?

Express Gratitude

Express Gratitude

Give thanks to the Lord,
for he is good;
his love endures forever.
Psalm 107:1

E very year just before or after New Year's Day my husband and I plan a special date. We go out to lunch or dinner and sit together for some time compiling a gratitude list for the year that is about to end. We have been doing this for more than a decade. Typically we end up with a list of seventy to eighty items for which we are grateful.

We don't do this because it is expected of us. We don't do this to impress anyone. We write a year-end gratitude list because this simple tradition does something powerful and wonderful in us. In fact, it is such a gift to us to write these lists that we look forward to this particular date probably more than any other date we have all year long.

Expressing gratitude is a simple thing to do. It is also a powerful thing to do. Whether we are saying "thank you" to God or to others, gratitude changes something inside us. Receiving the good gifts we are being given each day is an act of humility. It opens our eyes and our hearts to receive what we are being given.

For many years I found it very difficult to receive compliments or affirmations. I dismissed anything positive that might be said to me. I would avoid eye contact and wave people and their kind words away. At some point, however, I decided to actively change the way I responded to peoples' gifts of words to me. I started making an effort to stop myself from dismissing comments or from looking away. Instead, I began to look the person in the eye as they offered me a compliment or affirmation and to respond with two simple words: "Thank you." I decided that I didn't have to believe them or even enjoy the experience. It was my job to look them in the eyes and say "Thank you".

As I put this into practice I began to notice a couple of things happening to me. The first thing I noticed was that I was beginning to take in the gifts that others were offering me. I was beginning to feel differently about myself. It was not what we sometimes fear. I did not develop an over-inflated ego. Instead, I began to develop an awareness that I was seen and heard and valued—that I was loved.

The second thing I noticed was that the people who were offering me compliments or affirmations wanted to give me a gift. They wanted to offer me a blessing. I began to see these people more clearly whether they were strangers or close friends. As I received what they were giving me, I was able to see them and their kindness and beauty more clearly.

Both of these things changed me deeply. I became more present, more engaged, more available, more connected with others. I became more aware of being loved and valued and more capable of loving and valuing others. That is a lot to receive from the simple act of saying thank you.

But there is more. Expressing gratitude also leads to the experience of joy. Joy is often a direct outcome of expressions of gratitude. It is no wonder my husband and I look forward to our end-of-the-year-date.

But what about when life is difficult? What about those times when we are afraid or anxious or filled with grief? What role does expressing gratitude have then? I have found that it is helpful to express gratitude even in the middle of life's most difficult times. I am not saying that expressing gratitude is all we need to express at these times. Nor am I saying that expressing gratitude is some kind of magic cure-all in times when things are difficult. But expressing gratitude in the midst of life's difficulties is like letting a beam of light into a dark room. It helps us see that even in the hard times, we are being given gifts, we are being helped, we are loved. And that is a lot to see.

Seventeen days after I was diagnosed with breast cancer, I pulled an unused journal off my shelf and started to write prayers of gratitude. Already I could see that I was being given more gifts than I could keep track of. Gifts of support and love. Gifts of new perspectives. Gifts of deeper honesty and humility. Gifts of unexpected peace.

Gratitude sometimes begins with noticing things we don't always notice. The breath we draw. The body we rely on. The taste and texture of the food we eat. Each helper that comes into our lives in our times of need. The particular gifts they each bring. The places where our hearts are softening and becoming tender and open. The tears and the laughter we experience and share. The sacredness of it all. The presence of God in us, with us, in others around us.

Many of us unknowingly look away from the gifts being given to us, much like I once looked away when people offered me a compliment or an affirmation. This turning away from a gift is often the result of secretly believing that we do not deserve what we are being given. The gift we are being given does not match our internal sense of ourselves as unworthy to receive good gifts. But receiving good gifts is not about deserving something. Does an infant deserve our love and care? Of course. Even though an infant cannot do anything to earn this love? Of course. So when and how do we grow out of deserving love and care? We do not. We are valued. We are loved. Always.

When you don't know what to do…express gratitude.

Questions for reflection and discussion

1. Make a gratitude list, acknowledging the gifts you have been given in this time of difficulty.

2. What thoughts and feelings do you have as you look at this list?

Stay Open to Joy

Stay Open to Joy

You turned my wailing into dancing;
you removed my sackcloth
and clothed me with joy.
Psalm 30:11

I learned that I had cancer on a Thursday afternoon. The next morning I was planning to meet with a friend for breakfast. We have been meeting regularly for more than twenty three years. This particular Friday morning was to be our Christmas celebration. I had called her the night before to let her know about the diagnosis, but we didn't talk long because we knew we would have time together the next morning and I had many other calls to make.

I can't remember the Christmas present that she gave me that morning. Or the one I gave to her. But I do remember the words she wrote in her card. They were a soothing ointment to my raw nerves. They were especially powerful because they came from someone who had some credibility. This friend is a survivor of breast cancer, colon cancer and much else in life. Here is what she wrote:

> Dear Juanita,
> Have a wonderful Christmas with your family—enjoy every moment! In the weeks and months ahead may you experience the power of Jesus' presence in your life—light in moments of darkness, peace in the face of fear, courage in the unknown, love and security in the embrace of family and friends and joy in living.
> I love you.

The words that stayed with me the most through the following months were: "Joy in living." I asked my friend about them when I first read the card. "Yes, joy," she responded. "While I drove here to meet you I was praying to be shown the joy that God has for me today. I ask for this every day."

Joy was not exactly the first thing on my mind that morning, but I knew that my friend knew what she was talking about. She radiates joy. You can feel the warmth and light of genuine joy just being with her.

But joy did not come to me that morning, even though I was aware of feeling gratitude for the gifts I was already receiving. I was feeling more shock and anxiety than anything else.

But the joy did come. And when it came, it almost always came as a surprise.

Sometimes joy seemed to come out of nowhere. It wrapped me up and filled me up when I least expected it. On other occasions joy came leaping out at me after I set aside time to express gratitude for the gifts I was being given. Most amazingly of all, joy sometimes appeared after my deepest outpourings of grief. It was as if God literally did what the psalmist describes, as if God, at times, turned my wailing into dancing and removed my sackcloth to clothe me with joy.

I think there is actually an important connection between these things. I think the reason we sometimes experience joy after the expression of gratitude and grief is that expressions of gratitude and expressions of grief both ground us in the truth and open our hearts. Gratitude and grief are both vulnerable states. They are states of grace. They are moments when we let down our defenses a bit, when we soften, when we are receptive to God's tender mercies in ways that might not be possible in the more ordinary moments of life.

Something happens in those moments of receptivity. I believe that God is always available to us—pouring life and love and peace and light and joy into our lives. When the soil of our hearts is defended and hard, however, the rain runs off. It is not received so it cannot nourish us. But when our hearts are softened by expressions of gratitude and grief, the sweet rain of God's Presence is able to flow into us, nourishing and blessing us.

The connection between joy and grief is made explicit in a frequently misused text from the book of James: "Consider it pure joy whenever you face trials of many kinds" (James 1:2). The truth is I have never particularly liked this text. It sounds like pretending, like putting a good face on things, like some romantic, idealized but completely impractical notion. It doesn't feel real. I have heard far too many religious people talk as if God expects us to always look happy, even blissful. But I know that the wisdom of Scripture also teaches us to grieve and to be honest.

So where does the joy come from? It certainly doesn't come from pretending or from trying to be cheerful. It seems that the joy comes from being open to seeing that something is happening that is bigger than we are. That our difficulties, which occur for all sorts of reasons, always hold out gifts to us. They offer to challenge us. They offer to change us.

This is how this text from James says it: "Count it pure joy, my brothers, whenever you face trials of any kind, because you know that the testing of your faith develops perseverance. Perseverance must finish its work so that you may be mature and complete, not lacking anything" (James 1:2-4).

The journey to joy is like climbing a steep mountain. At least two things happen during the hike. One is that as we keep hiking, we grow stronger. We can't see it but our spiritual bones and muscles and heart and lungs grow stronger. The other thing that happens is that as we get closer to the top, we begin to see a view that we otherwise would not have seen. We see the bigger picture.

Something else happens on the climb as well. Because the ascent is so difficult we are likely to see that we cannot do it alone. We need companionship. We need help. In the middle of struggling up the steep slope we find that we are not alone. Sometimes we are being guided. Sometimes we are even carried. By God. By others.

These gifts (stronger spiritual muscles, bigger perspectives, knowing we are not alone) all serve to deepen our faith. The joy that emerges out of difficult circumstances is that we gain a greater capacity to trust that in all circumstances we are held and safe, that we are known and loved.

Ultimately joy is about being loved. About knowing we are loved. About "remaining" (resting, living) in love.

It was in this way that the words "Count it pure joy whenever you face trials of many kinds," came to be real for me. Many days I did not feel joy, but as I was given grace to persevere, joy had a way of emerging over and over again.

Since the day I received the Christmas card from my friend, I have remembered often to pray, as she does, to be shown the joy God has for me each day. I recommend it. Pray to be shown joy, whatever your circumstances. Joy will come.

When you don't know what to do…stay open to joy.

Questions for reflection and discussion

1. What experiences have you had with joy during this or other times of difficulty?

2. What do you think was the source of this joy?

Make Room for Laughter

Make Room
for Laughter

There is a time for everything,
and a season for everything under heaven,
a time to weep and a time to laugh.
Ecclesiastes 3:1,4

Many years ago when I was first dating my husband, he made the comment that it might be good for me to learn to laugh more. At the time I was so serious about everything that I didn't really know what he was talking about. I have learned to lighten up over the years.

Of course, our problems are not laughing matters. A struggling marriage, a troubled teen, financial worries or a diagnosis of cancer are serious. Laughing is not usually the first thing a person thinks to do. In fact, laughing about these things may be inappropriate. But at some point, finding a way to have a good laugh can be a great help.

Humor releases those "feel good" chemicals in our brains and bodies. It helps restore perspective, and it can help us reconnect with our hope and joy.

One of the many challenges I faced after receiving a diagnosis of breast cancer was that I had to give up my estrogen and progesterone supplements. I had been taking a version of these two hormones for several years, and I greatly appreciated the reduction in forgetfulness, hot flashes, bone loss, insomnia and a list of other symptoms that they provided. Giving them up was difficult.

Several months after I had been without my friends Estrogen and Progesterone, I went with three of my fifty-something girl friends to *Menopause: the Musical.* We laughed and laughed as the four women on stage belted out songs about mind collapse and personal summers that are really a bummer. It was a good thing to laugh together at ourselves.

One of these friends has a great story she likes to tell about the first time she called the doctor about hormone replacement therapy. She told him that she had three symptoms. One was insomnia, another was hot flashes and...she forgot the third. "Memory problems?" he asked.

Not all humor is healing, of course. Humor that is used as a disguise for a put down or that comes at someone else's expense does not bring healing.

What is it that makes something funny and helpful? Playful surprise. The courage to be honest. The ability to identify with others. Freedom from shame about our common human problems.

But we don't have to be comedians to laugh in the midst of a difficult situation. It can be helpful to watch a funny movie or to listen to a stand-up comedian. Or to talk with a little kid and listen to their take on things. Or to read a funny book. Anything that helps us laugh can help ease our distress and help us heal.

Humor can even help us honor and remember someone with love. When I co-led a cancer support group we always set aside a full evening to reminisce when one of the group members died. Every time we did this it was a rich experience. We shared stories of the person who had died. We almost always cried together. And we almost always laughed together because almost always the person who had died had given us gifts of humor as they lived and died with their cancer. They had found those qualities of honesty and identification with others and freedom from shame that can allow humor to emerge. And, as a result, they had laughed at themselves. They had left this gift with us to share with each other as we remembered them.

One day my husband and I sat on a big rock at Laguna Beach

together. Our feet were on the wet sand. The waves were breaking at some distance from us and then sliding quietly closer to touch our toes. It was a quiet summer evening but we were not doing well. We were not happy with each other. So we sat there encircled by great beauty, depressed about life and about our relationship. Suddenly, out of nowhere a huge wave rose up and broke on top of us. We were drenched and shrieking in surprise. And laughing. The negative spell was broken. Our eyes and hearts opened. We laughed and we kept laughing. We were laughing at ourselves. At how wet we were. At how pouty we had been. At our inability to see the gifts all around of us.

Later, as I reflected on that moment, it felt like God had playfully splashed water on us, as if coaxing us to lighten up and open up. It felt like God had used the element of surprise to help us laugh. There was still hard work that needed to be done, but God's playfulness was well-timed and helped us heal.

Whatever joy or sorrow we are experiencing, whatever challenge or opportunity is being handed us, it is a relief to come to the place where we can let go and laugh.

When you don't know what to do…make room for laughter.

Questions for reflection and discussion

1. What humor have you enjoyed during difficult times?

2. How has humor been helpful to you?

Celebrate Each Day

Celebrate
Each Day

This is the day that the Lord has made;
we will rejoice and be glad in it.
Psalm 118:24

T he kind of cancer I had was not life-threatening, but because of the diagnosis, I came to know more directly than ever before that I am not immune from catastrophic illness and death. With this refresher course in personal mortality came a heightened capacity to taste the sweetness of life.

Life is often hard. And mundane. But sometimes we are able to notice the gifts a day holds. Big gifts and little gifts. These moments of noticing and taking in the gifts of life can transform both the difficult and the mundane into experiences of grace.

When we are reminded that our days are numbered, there can be times when we are able to see the blessedness of life. We are able to see the amazing gift it is to be breathing, talking, walking here on earth.

I had a few such unexpected moments after being diagnosed. These moments had been described to me earlier by a good friend who is a cancer survivor as "moments of clarity."

One day while I was walking from my office to a nearby restaurant for lunch, I felt like I stepped into a different dimension. Colors were suddenly more brilliant. The air felt magically charged. I felt stunningly alive. Moments of clarity like this did not last long or come often. But they were touchstones. They reminded me of how little we see and how little we know of the glories of this life and the life to come. These moments of clarity felt like moments of heaven on earth. Perhaps they are little glimpses of heaven. Perhaps they are glimpses of the presence of heaven here with us all the time. Whatever they are, they are gifts to be savored.

One of the impacts of these moments was that for several months after my experience with cancer I would wake up in the morning and look at the calendar hanging on our bedroom wall. As I looked at that day's date, I would feel a wash of awe that I had been given the gift of this new day. Before I thought about what the day might hold or all I needed to attend to, I would first experience this gentle sensation pass through me. June 5. August 20. October 15. Whatever the day might be, I would look at the number on the calendar like I was looking at something that glimmered, something sacred, something filled with light and air and kindness, a personal gift beautifully wrapped, delivered at my doorstep.

I did not try to do this. It just happened. But the experience was so pleasant that I sometimes looked back at the calendar a second time, not to note the date again, but to feel that sense of blessed awe pour out on me and move through me one more time.

Sometimes celebrating each day may not look like much of a celebration. When we are physically ill or in emotional distress, just getting through the day, one day at a time may be all we can do.

The wisdom of living one day at a time is wisdom that Jesus taught. The Gospels record Jesus teaching us to trust God to provide for us each day. Jesus invites us to consider the lilies of the field and the birds of the air, how they do not toil, yet they have everything they need and more. He goes on to challenge us to consider if worrying can add one hour to our lives. Then he invites us to let go of all worry about tomorrow because we can trust that God who made us and values us will provide for us (Matthew 6:25-34).

Today is where we are. Today is what we have been given. Today we will be given the help and strength and grace we need for whatever the day brings. Life comes to us, a sweet gift, one day at a time.

When we are anxious and afraid, it is often because we are imagining difficulties that may arise the next day or the next week or the next year. When we find our minds time traveling in this way, we do well to come back to this moment, this day. We can trust that whatever comes our way tomorrow will come wrapped in the grace and strength we will need at the time. Today is the day we have been given, and in whatever way we can, we can honor the gift of today and even celebrate it.

Sometimes it helps to find simple ways to celebrate the gift of each day of life. Our celebration might be in the form of a prayer of gratitude for the day in the morning or in the evening, or both. Or it might be the celebration of standing and lifting our arms each morning in a gesture of receptivity. Or of lifting our voice in song. Or making music. Or expressing gratitude to the people in our life for the ordinary ways they bless us. Or lighting a candle and observing a moment of quiet awareness.

Each day is holy. Each day is a gift. May you find ways to celebrate.

When you don't know what to do…celebrate each day.

Questions for reflection and discussion

1. What gifts have you noticed today?

2. What might help you celebrate the gift of each day?

Let Yourself Be Carried

Let Yourself
Be Carried

He tends his flock like a shepherd;
He gathers the lambs in his arms
and carries them close to his heart.
Isaiah 40:11

One summer we took a trip to Maine to visit family. While there, we went to an island off the coast to spend a few days hiking. On one of our hikes, my husband commented on the fact that the trail we were on was no longer a trail but a long series of boulders we had to scramble over. Seconds after this observation, a tree root which had grown across the boulder he was crossing snapped under his foot, twisting his ankle and sending him sliding. As he landed we heard a second snap, this time it was the sound of his ankle and leg breaking in three places.

We were on an island which had no hospital or medical facilities. We were several miles away from the dock and the boat that could carry us back to the mainland. My husband needed to get to that dock. There was no way that he could move on his own. He would need to be carried.

One of our group went to the nearest cottage and explained our dilemma. Before we knew it, a group of volunteers from the island had gathered around my husband. They had come with a stretcher and their willingness to carry him several miles to the boat. One of them, a nurse, traveled all the way to the mainland with us where an ambulance waited to take us to the hospital.

My husband had no choice. If he wanted to get the help he needed, he had to let himself be carried. With a great deal of grace, he accepted the gifts of time, energy and care given by these strangers who voluntarily offered to help in this time of need.

There are many ways that we need to be carried during difficult times in our lives. Sometimes we need to be carried physically by others who offer their time and strength. Sometimes we need to be carried emotionally or spiritually by others who offer their love and their prayers.

One of the most moving dynamics of the cancer support group I co-led, years before my own diagnosis of cancer, was the many ways in which the group members carried each other. They called each other. They wrote notes of encouragement to each other. And they prayed for each other. Often, one of the members would comment about a season in which it had been impossible for them to pray for themselves, either because they were too spent, too discouraged, or too ill from their treatments. They would frequently comment during these times about the amazing experience of feeling carried by the love and prayers of other members of the group.

This experience of being carried by other people's love and prayers happened for me as I walked through the weeks and months of my experience with cancer. And it happened for me as I walked for years through the painful process of healing from childhood trauma. And it happened as we walked through healing as a family when our oldest son got help for his drug addiction. Through each of these life crises, many people said they were praying for me, and did pray for me, and for us as a family. I often felt a sense of peace and rest and even of floating that was beyond understanding, except as pure gift. It was the gift of being carried in times when I could not walk on my own.

It is easy enough to say that we will pray for each other. But, when we really do, I am convinced that something happens. Some have described praying as participating in the powerful current of God's healing energy. As co-creators or co-workers with God, our prayers add to that healing current. Perhaps our prayers are like the arms that carried my husband's stretcher, arms that remind us that we are always being carried in the arms of God.

Scripture tells us that God is like a shepherd who gathers his lambs in his arms and carries them close to his heart. We are God's lambs. We are always carried close to God's tender heart. I do not know exactly what happens when other people pray for us, but I am convinced that these prayers offer us an opportunity to be carried—to be supported. And they provide a tangible reminder that we are always being carried by God's tender mercies, close to God's heart.

Perhaps what we need most is to receive the love, support and prayer which we are offered, and then to let ourselves be carried.

When you don't know what to do…let yourself be carried.

Questions for reflection and discussion

1. Who is caring for you and praying for you during this difficult time?

2. Describe a time when you have had a sense of being carried close to God's heart.

Be Who You Are

Be Who
You Are

One day while driving along a familiar road, I found myself accelerating through a yellow light. Everyone behind me had to stop, and I felt for an instant that I had "won." It was as if we had all been racing and I had just pulled ahead and beat everyone. I enjoyed my small victory.

But my pride didn't last long. In order to make it through the yellow light, I had stepped on the gas. As a result, I flew right past a police officer. Soon his flashing lights were in my rear view mirror. From pride to embarrassment in one quick moment.

As I pulled to a stop and waited for the policeman to come to my window, I reflected on the attitude that I had been caught up in—the fleeting sense that I was in competition with other drivers, and the pleasure I experienced of making it through the light while others were left behind. I was not happy with myself. I could see the unnecessary competitiveness in my spirit, and the small, private display of pride. As a result, I saw the presence of the officer as a potential gift.

Of course I felt awful about getting a ticket. I didn't like the idea of paying a fine or of having this on my record. But I could see that I needed an attitude adjustment, and that this ticket offered me an opportunity to reflect and make some changes.

I don't think that I got the ticket to teach me a lesson. I got the ticket because I was speeding. But the ticket did provide me with an opportunity to let go of my pride—again. It gave me a moment to observe that if I had been operating my life at a saner pace,

I would have slowed down and stopped at the yellow light. If I wasn't half consciously believing I was in competition with other drivers, I would have been making safer, more respectful choices.

What the speeding ticket offered me was a reminder that I am one among many drivers. A reminder that together, as a community of drivers, we have a need to care for each other's safety and well-being. That humble respectfulness and sense of community is what I needed to embrace as I let go of a sense of competition and of concern primarily for myself.

Years later, the diagnosis of cancer offered me a very similar gift. Cancer allowed me to experience in a very direct way that I am an ordinary mortal. Like all mortals, I get sick. I am growing old. I am going to die. And like all of us, I need the help and support of other people.

In the weeks of waiting for a full diagnosis I realized that I was being allowed to experience the truth of my mortality. It was a bitter-sweet experience. As a result of this direct, visceral encounter, all the non-essentials of life momentarily fell away. All the superficial ways by which I might measure myself and my life, lost all meaning and interest to me.

What mattered was no longer trying to "look good" in some way, or wanting to succeed in some way. What mattered were the simplest of truths. I came from God. I belong to God. I am loved by God. I am always with God, and God is always with me. I will return to God. I am held by God now and always. I am one of God's many beloved children. Together we belong to God. And we belong to each other. The bitter taste of mortality lead to a reconnection with these grace-full truths.

None of us is better or more important. We are all valued, cherished, loved. Knowing this makes it possible to stop clinging to self-sufficiency. Knowing this makes it possible to die to our false selves, our defenses, our pretenses, our masks. It makes it possible for us to be who we really are—free from any need to prove ourselves, or to gain recognition. We don't have to struggle to "be somebody" because we are already somebody. We are God's beloved children. To know this is to have everything.

When you don't know what to do…be who you are.

Questions for reflection and discussion

1. What impact have your experiences of difficulties in life had on your pride?

2. In what way has this been freeing for you?

Know That You Are Loved

Know That You Are Loved

I trust in your unfailing love.
Psalm 13:5

After my second surgery my husband and I spent a week at the beach. Both of us needed to recuperate from the many weeks of uncertainty and strain. It was the week of our thirty-seventh wedding anniversary. So we needed to both rest and celebrate.

We were no longer waiting for results. We were no longer anticipating the possibility of radiation therapy. We knew the cancer had been removed and that I did not have to go through radiation. I was done. I was cancer free.

We rested well that week. It was the middle of March, a few weeks before Easter break, so the beach was empty most of the time. Beautiful. And quiet.

On the last full day that we were there, we were blessed with a rain storm that lasted only a few hours. When the sky cleared, it was a deep, brilliant blue, strewn with an array of white clouds that were turning golden. It was too beautiful to stay inside, so I went out for a long walk.

While I walked my heart turned to God. I was full of gratitude and awe. I had no words. The sky said what I could not. The storm had come. It had baptized us with water. It had purified the air. Then it cleared, leaving a few clouds behind to reflect the light of the sun. It was peaceful now. Everything felt blessed. And hushed.

As I walked, I found myself looking at the sand, scanning for a rock I might save. I am a bit of a scavenger for unusually shaped rocks, but I reminded myself that rocks were not the agenda that day. They paled in comparison to the drama of the light show going on in the sky above me and on the ocean and sand in front of me.

After walking for a while I stopped and stood for a time, marveling at the gold and silver light in the sky and the wonderful way the light was reflected on the water and the sand. I was in state of quiet awe.

After standing in that spot for a while, I glanced down at my feet before moving on. There, right in front of me, was a smooth, flat rock in the perfect shape of a heart. I picked it up and held it as my eyes brimmed with tears.

The One who created the vast beauty I had been enjoying was the same God who had cared for me with such tender mercy. There was something about holding this rock in my hand that provided a tangible symbol for the many experiences of God's provision that had graced the recent months. I found myself talking to God in the simple words of a child. "Thank you, thank you, thank you." I whispered. "You always help me and take care of me. And you tell me in a hundred ways that you love me. Thank you. I love you."

I thought for a moment about our grandson at Christmas when he was two and a half years old. With each gift he unwrapped he would say to the person who had given it to him, "You gave it me?" And when that person said, "Yes," he threw himself at them, wrapped his arms around them and said, "Oh, kank you!"

That is what my heart was saying to God, "You gave it me? All the gifts of peace and guidance and help? You gave it me, God? Thank you."

I carried the rock home. I think of it as an I-love-you rock from God. It is a tangible symbol, a physical reminder, a visualization of how intimately and tenderly I am loved—of how intimately and tenderly we all are loved.

Now, when I pick up the heart-shaped rock and hold it in my hand I am reminded of all the years of healing, all the gifts of love God has given to me. "I love you," God says over and over. "Thank you," I whisper back. "Thank you."

May God grant you the capacity to trust that most fundamental of all truths: you are loved. Always. Faithfully. Unconditionally. Tenderly. Intimately.

When you don't know what to do…know that you are loved.

Questions for reflection and discussion

1. What difficulties have you had believing that you are loved by God?

2. What has helped you to trust God's love for you?

Footnotes

1. Monica Brown, "Into Your Hands," from *Holy Ground: Mantras and Chants for Reflection and Prayer*, ©2000 Emmaus Productions, www.emmausproductions.com.

2. Rachel Remen *Kitchen Table Wisdom* (Riverhead Trade, 2006).

3. Henri Nouwen, *The Path of Waiting* (New York, NY: Crossroad, 1995)

4. Margaret Bullit-Jonas, *Christ's Passion, Our Passions* (Cambridge, MA: Cowley Publications, 2002), 7.

5. Sue Monk Kidd, *When the Heart Waits* (San Francisco, CA: Harper San Francisco, 1990), 13.

6. Elizabeth Gilbert, *Eat, Pray, Love* (New York, N.Y.: Penguin Books, 2007), 15-16.

7. Thomas Merton, *Contemplative Prayer* (New York. N.Y.: Image Books, 1969), 29-30.

8. Belleruth Naparstek, *Successful Surgery - Health Journey*. Available at www.healthjourneys.com.

For additional resources we encourage you to
visit the web site of the
National Association for Christian Recovery!

You will find online discussion groups,
an extensive library, online workshops,
a daily meditation by email (taken from *Rooted
in God's Love* by Dale and Juanita Ryan)
and lots of other good stuff.

www.nacronline.com

For other books
by Juanita Ryan visit:

http://www.nacronline.com/nacr-store/books

For Bible studies by Juanita Ryan visit:

http://www.nacronline.com/nacr-store/bible-stud-
ies-by-dale-and-juanita-ryan